A LIFETIME'S NON-ORDINARY EVENTS

A MODIFIED AUTOBIOGRAPHY

Richard F. Ward

Order this book online at www.trafford.com
or email orders@trafford.com

Most Trafford titles are also available at major online book retailers.

Print information available on the last page.

ISBN: 978-1-4269-1074-6 (sc)

Trafford rev. 06/01/2015

North America & international
toll-free: 1 888 232 4444 (USA & Canada)
fax: 812 355 4082

This work is dedicated to the memory of my wife
Lu Ward and her first cousin Thelma L. Martin
who made the meeting with Lu possible

OTHER BOOK BY AUTHOR:

South & West of the Capitol Dome

v

INTRODUCTION

In about the year 1980, I began recording the non-ordinary events, people met and places visited in my life. Eventually I looked back into my past life to recount events, people and places which came to mind in the earlier years. As the years rolled by, I had assembled a list of 171 items which I consider unusual or non-ordinary in my lifetime.

My next step in the evolution of this work was to elaborate on each of the parts - to expand on each of the one or two line statements. When assembled, I realized it provided an autobiography, albeit different from the usual biography, of my life. Hopefully, the treatment will render the human story more entertaining to the average reader. Having reached the middle of my octogenarian decade, perhaps a better perspective of the life can thus be obtained.

But the reader's entertainment is the effect I hope to impart. If this should ensue, the effort shall not have been in vain.

BORN ON THE "NEW YORK ISLAND" - MANHATTAN, NY, NY. - 1923

On 200th Street in Manhattan also named Dyckman St., in what is now Inwood Hill Park, my mom, Minnie Meier Ward, gave me birth. The date was June 29, 1923. The hospital located there - the Jewish Memorial Hospital - subsequently moved to Broadway and 196th Street in Manhattan. The nonsectarian hospital moved to the new location, maybe two miles from the old location, in 1936.

Of course, I remember nothing of my birth, but when I walked around the neighborhood as a youngster I do remember the old hospital as being an old and dark castle-like structure, high and overlooking the Hudson River. In 1940/41 when I was 17 years old, I remember being treated at the hospital on Broadway when I was mysteriously stricken with Bell's Palsy. The malady left the left side of my face paralyzed, i.e., I was unable to move the muscles on that side of my face. Apparently, in 1940, they were unfamiliar with the ailment. I had to visit the hospital weekly, as I recall, to have mild electric current applied on my left forehead. The treatment was uncomfortable but not overly painful. I don't believe the current application helped at the time, although the paralysis has very slowly, over a period of decades, virtually disappeared.

Inwood Hill Park is now a large, wild wooded area with paved paths snaking through it. It's situated at the northwestern corner of Manhattan Island, also called New York County. I spent many an hour in the park playing ball in the attached ball park and walking my dog Teddy through the woods.

SAILED ON HUDSON RIVER DAY LINE BOAT
TO KINGSTON, NY. - 1933

I sailed on Hudson River Day Line boats numerous times. The boats were named the ALEXANDER HAMILTON, ROBERT FULTON, DE WITT CLINTON, HENDRICK HUDSON, PETER STYVESANT and maybe some other famous names in New York history.

I must have been 10 years old, or maybe 13, when, for some reason, my parents had me sail on one of the boats from Kingston to NYC alone or maybe with my sister, 6 (or 9) year old Marian. As I recall, my mom said I should go out on deck as soon as I handed over my ticket so she could see me. She also told me to say I was a bit younger than I was so I could travel half-price. I remember telling the ticket-taker my correct age unfortunately. He detained me and I'm sure mom must have wondered or worried about what happened. Thankfully, the boat attendant let me sail on the boat. I scrambled to the outside railing in time to see mom as we left Kingston, NY. Dad or perhaps Aunt Mary met me at the New York City end (125th St. in Manhattan). I don't think parents would do things like that these days in the 21st Century. It must have been somewhat traumatic for me as I still remember the event so many years later.

The trip itself is great along the beautiful and historic Hudson.

Hudson River Day Line Boat

PLAYED STICKBALL ON NEW YORK CITY NEIGHBORHOOD STREETS - 1935

Much of our play as young teenagers in New York was done in the streets. Later, more parks were built for kids to play in, particularly when Parks Commissioner Robert Moses was in charge under Mayor Fiorello LaGuardia, the "Little Flower". But in the early days, the streets were the ideal playground. They had space -- yes, some cars but not like it is today. If our local street was too filled with parked cars, we would go to another part of town where the traffic was sparser. The streets had built in bases -- the manhole covers and sewer gratings and the "field" was extensive, at least from home plate through centerfield.

No uniforms were required, but, of course, we needed bats and balls. For bats we obtained old broom handles, sawed off at the proper length. I liked the handles, now "sticks", that were shaped somewhat like a real baseball bat, i. e., thicker at both ends and rather thin just above where one would grip it. When you hit a ball with this stick just right (in the sweet spot), it would travel fast and far. And the ball? Our favorite ball was the rubber "Spalding" which we some how mangled into "Spaldeen".

Baseball rules applied, of course. If we had lots of players, we could get 9 men on each side. If not, we cut out a couple of outfielders and one or two infielders. We chose up sides by alternating choices, after determining who would choose first, by putting fist-over-fist on a stick. The last one to hold it firmly would choose first and naturally select the best player in his estimation. We'd use chalk on the street to keep score, although it seemed to me the score wasn't that important (it's how you play the game - the Olympic Spirit?). The pitcher would throw the ball to the batter on one bounce; no balls and strikes were tallied.

Those were the things I remembered in "those good old days".

SOLD, WITH SISTER MARIAN'S HELP, SATURDAY EVENING POST AND LADIES HOME JOURNAL MAGAZINES AT 207TH STREET SUBWAY STOP - 1938

Magazine representatives would come around the neighborhood streets in their big black cars and entice us to make some money and earn some coupons (greenies and brownies) for neat prizes. I'd get this stack of SATURDAY EVENING POST's and LADIES HOME JOURNAL's one day. Marian and I would head for the subway stop and peddle the literature. She did pretty good since she was 4 years my junior and very blond.

We did very well for awhile. I don't recall why we eventually ceased, perhaps it was illegal on city property or perhaps we just grew tired of the endeavor. Anyway it was fun while it lasted. In the beginning, we weren't given too many to sell, but as sales picked up we were given more and more. Eventually, the load became too burdensome.

RODE THROUGH 'NEW ENGLAND STORM OF 1938' - 1938

In September of this year, in the years before storms were given names, a monster hurricane moved through the northeast, primarily New England, but also New York City. The final count of deaths related to the storm was between five and six hundred.

It happened in the middle of the week. I can recall going to school at George Washington High. Normally, we would walk maybe a couple of miles from our apartments in upper Manhattan to the school on Washington Heights. In inclement weather, however, we (I usually walked with my school chum Kenny Koehler) would take the "old" subway, the IRT which would have its stations closer to our homes and, at the other end, to the school than the "new" subway, the IND.

The IRT was for the most part underground, like a subway should be. But because of topography and the fact that it was built 35 or 40 years earlier, the train came out into the open at 200th Street, a stop before the stop we used to get on and off the train.

So, on the bad weather afternoon of September 21 after school let out for the day, we took the train home. At the 200th Street station the train came out into the open. As we rode from 200th Street to 207th Street, our destination, the train encountered fierce, buffeting winds - so much so that the whole train or at least the car in which we were riding lurched perceptively from side to side. It was a scary feeling. We were maybe 25 feet off the ground on elevated tracks. It was very unusual to be rocked from side to side like that in a moving subway car. I still remember the incident. We soon arrived safely at our destination thankfully - a little scared but none the worse for wear.

VISITED NEW YORK WORLD'S FAIR
NUMEROUS TIMES - 1939

In 1939, I'm all of 15/16 years of age. But a big deal occurs in New York City, even by New York standards - The New York World's Fair. It meant taking the subway to 59th Street, Manhattan, transferring to the Queens line and traveling to the Fair Grounds at Flushing Meadows, a long trip.

But it was exciting going through the entrance and seeing all these strange looking buildings and modernistic erections. There were the government buildings with the USA building at the head of the government area. The major countries - the UK, France, Spain - had erected beautiful edifices and of course the interiors where more or less jaw-dropping.

Then there was the NYC building. I remember, after 70 years, the moving train of seats that took us on a journey all around the city which was a giant model laid out below. There's Central Park. Look, the George Washington Bridge (all of 8 or 9 years old), Coney Island and Brooklyn, midtown Manhattan dominated by the Empire State Building (tallest building in the world then), the Wall Street area of Manhattan with its Woolworth Building (once the tallest), the Bronx with the zoological park (the Bronx Zoo) and botanical gardens and so many other familiar landmarks too numerous to enumerate.

But the commercial area of the fair was probably the ultimate destination for most people. There were General Motors, Ford and Chrysler (free car rides and glimpses of the new lines). There was American Telephone & Telegraph where one could make a telephone call anywhere in the country - for free! Kodak showed beautiful monster-sized photographs, the petroleum industry had a working oil well, as I recall, and General Electric produced a giant electric spark maybe 20 feet long. Wow!

And last but not least, the food industry. Heinz, Beech-nut. Here one could get free food with a little persistence by standing on line and waiting your turn. Actually, there were lines at just about every exhibit, particularly if the rewards were extra enticing.

Finally, there was Billy Rose's Aquacade where a big swim show was performed. Since this required an entrance fee, I never went. I said 'finally', but actually there were so many other things to see and people to meet (I got Leo Durocher's autograph in one of the exhibits, for example). I don't think you could ever say 'finally' about this spectacular and wondrous collection of human activity. I, and usually my sister with me, went numerous times and we were awed by what we saw. As kids, we never stayed late into the evening when the magnificent "Fire and Water Show" took place with fireworks and water jets on the lagoon.

And in the center of it all were the Trylon and Perisphere -- maybe the way the future will look in the 21st Century.

TOOK THE "A" TRAIN - 1940

If the line is good enough for Duke Ellington, it's good enough for me. Of course, one of his musical hits was the song with that title in the present tense.

The "A" train was a part of the "new" subway as we called it then - the Independent System or IND. There were also the Interborough Rapid Transit or IRT and the Brooklyn Manhattan Transit or BMT Systems. The IRT was the oldest system starting operations in the early 1900's. The IRT and the IND both had stops in my neighborhood in uptown Manhattan - Inwood, north of Washington Heights.

Living in uptown Manhattan and working in the midtown or downtown parts of the island, I rode the IND's "A" train many, many times. The train had stops every 10 to 20 blocks or so, but it completely bypassed the 66 blocks between 125h St. and 59th Street - the Central Park area. Thus, one could go on the "A" train from its northern terminus at 207th Street near where we lived on 204th Street to midtown Manhattan in less than half an hour.

Of course, the NY subway system has been completely revised as far as system and name changes are concerned. IND, IRT and BMT have been integrated into one vast but efficient system. City folk really have no need for automobile transportation. I, for instance, didn't have a car until I moved to Washington, DC when I was almost 30 years old. I read many a newspaper article while traveling on the "A" train.

As to the link between the "A" train and the Duke, the train ran through Harlem in NY where he usually displayed his preeminent musical talents.

GRADUATED FROM GEORGE WASHINGTON HIGH SCHOOL, NYC - 1941

Unlike college, you could graduate from high school in January in NYC, rather than June, if you met all the academic requirements. I was fairly proud of myself for getting a diploma in a General Academic Course. My mom stressed attaining a good attendance record for school and it probably paid off.

But an odd thing happened at this time. Maybe a month or two before graduation I came down with a strange ailment, as previously mentioned. One morning I woke up with a paralysis of the movement muscles on the left side of my face. I only had half a smile and I couldn't wink my left eye or raise my left eyebrow. In fact I couldn't close my left eyelid satisfactorily. At the time, I don't remember the doctors calling the affliction by the name I eventually learned it to be, Bell's Palsy.

Everyone figured I had caught a draft in the cold weather to account for its occurrence. I wondered if the impending graduation might account for it. I was a shy youngster, perhaps excessively so. I lacked some of the sociability skills that church attendance might impart. At any rate, I didn't attend my own high school graduation. Of course, attendance wasn't a requirement to obtain the diploma.

Almost two years later when I was inducted into the armed services and took the standard achievement and placement tests, I was placed in the Army Signal Corps. I always felt that my academic schooling helped me attain a more cerebral less physical army activity in WW II.

As to the Bell's Palsy, the hospital gave me weekly mild electric shock treatments on my left forehead for maybe several months. I did not feel that the electric shock therapy helped my affliction, although the lack of movement in my left-side facial muscles slowly, over a period of months and years, disappeared. Tiny vestiges of it, however, are still present.

When I went to a George Washington High school reunion some 50 years later, one guy remembered me probably from class. I didn't remember him. He did give me an opportunity to get my class photo. It shows no facial skewing although it may have been taken before the palsy had set in.

WORKED AS SHIPPING CLERK FOR LUCIEN LELONG PERFUMES, MADISON AVENUE, NYC - 1941

Lucien Lelong conducted its perfume shipping operations from 585 Madison Avenue in the heart of midtown Manhattan. It was a sweet smelling job.

About the only memory I have of the job, besides the location, was a pigeon flight! Our location was high in a tall building, maybe on the 10th or 12th story. We occupied the entire floor. At the back of the office where the shipping room was, was a balcony/fire escape. Employees could eat their brown-bagged lunches out there.

One noontime I came out and scared a pigeon off the railing. He flew and soared to another fire escape in a building across from us whose front was on Park Avenue, the next street to the east. It took him maybe 10 or 12 seconds. It made me think: If I wanted to go to the same place that bird had gone, I would have to go through the office, out the entrance, over to the elevator, wait for the elevator, go down to the building lobby, out into Madison Avenue, walk around the corner on 53rd Street, around another corner on Park Avenue, into the proper building, up the elevator to the proper floor, into the correct office and, finally, out on the back fire escape. So, a trip of 10 seconds for the pigeon would take me 15 minutes or so!

I guess this proves what a marvelous thing flight is, or how, in some respects, humanity has outwitted itself in the realm of point-to-point transportation. Perhaps I should have stuck to munching on my sandwich or packing, labeling and shipping perfume bottles.

LEFT THEATER AFTER SEEING WW I MOVIE "SERGEANT YORK" ON AFTERNOON WE HEARD PEARL HARBOR, HAWAII WAS ATTACKED - 1941

I went to the movies alone that Sunday afternoon to see "Sergeant York". When I came out squinting and blinking into the bright sunshine I seemed to sense something strange and different. I can't put my finger on the feeling. Little did I know at that time an event had occurred or was occurring that would change my life completely, as well as the lives of millions of other Americans and indeed millions of lives of people throughout the world.

After a ten minute walk I got home to hear the news from my folks - Japan had bombed Pearl Harbor and the Navy ships docked there. It seemed incredulous. Even though the war had been raging in Europe for two years (part of it a "phony" war because of inactivity), the USA had steered clear of it. But not now. President Franklin D. Roosevelt declared war on the "Axis" powers one or two days later, the "Axis" being Japan, Germany and Italy. The individuals in those countries most responsible were Premier Tojo in Japan, Nazi Chancellor Hitler in Germany and Fascist Dictator Mussolini in Italy.

A little over a year later I was inducted into the Army and less than a year after that I was in Europe. Seven months later I landed in Normandy (Omaha beach) a month after D-Day.

A year and a half later I was honorably discharged and within months, going to New York University under the GI Bill of Rights. After graduation in three and a half years, I was able to pursue a career with the federal government with the Census Bureau and, later, the Army Department, primarily in a personnel capacity.

But a decision made in Tokyo, Japan set the course for my life. And on that sunny December day, after identifying with Sergeant York in WW I in the movie theater, it was beginning to dawn on me.

DELIVERED BIWEEKLY, BY BROOKLYN BRIDGE TRAIN FROM MANHATTAN, TYPEWRITER PARTS TO NYC REPAIR SHOP BENEATH THE BRIDGE IN BROOKLYN - 1942

I worked for Ames Supply Co. which supplied typewriter parts and services all over downtown and midtown Manhattan. The company had its office and shop on Ames Street just 2 or 3 blocks from NY's City Hall in downtown Manhattan.

I had one route delivering parts which happened to make a wide loop around the Empire State building in midtown Manhattan. Typewriter repair shops were scattered all over the main part of town keeping the essential and ubiquitous typewriter in good working order. This, of course, was before the days of the computer. I loved this route. Some shops were directly on the streets. Others required a circuitous journey through retail outlets or were high up in the tall buildings requiring elevator trips. But I sporadically had a view of the magnificent Empire State Building in my loopy trip.

But the biweekly trip to the NYC repair shop beneath the Brooklyn Bridge was almost fun. I'd gather up my orders and head for the train which would carry me across the East River to Brooklyn over the Brooklyn Bridge. The famous bridge in 1942 was 59 years old. Now it's 125 years old and counting and still doing its job faithfully - transporting people and things between the two NYC boroughs. To me this route in my job was a mini-vacation. The only downside was that the valise I carried filled with parts and supplies could get quite heavy. Sometimes I think it helped put a little unwanted curvature in my spine.

THRILLED AS GENE KRUPA'S BAND ROSE FROM THE PIT AT PARAMOUNT THEATER, NYC - 1942

In between jobs, and I had more than a few shipping clerk and delivery jobs, I saw a matinee movie at the Paramount Theater on Times Square in NY. I don't remember the movie, but I do remember very vividly that they had live entertainment between showings. I guess the most popular entertainment were the "big bands".

We all still remember the names; Glenn Miller, Tommy Dorsey, Benny Goodman, Harry James, Gene Krupa, Count Basie, Duke Ellington, Artie Shaw, Les Brown and so many others -- both older and newer. In those days we most likely called them swing bands. The term "big band" came later, to distinguish them from the less labor intensive musical combination.

But one day before the war, I saw some show at the theater. I'll never forget after the motion picture ended and the giant Wurlitzer organ finished its transitional introduction, the sound of Gene Krupa's theme song could be heard. The first strains were somewhat muted, but as the whole band rose higher from the pit on a great stage, the music was unmistakable. And when the moving stage had reached the level of the regular stage and the music was at full volume, there was Gene pounding away at the skins giving the band the rhythm and beat which characterized the Krupa sound.

The rising from the pit was somewhat of a surprise to me. It sent shivers up and down my spine. And, of course, the familiar music and beat only added to the memorable effect. I know I'll never forget the experience. And the sound made by 15 or 20 expert musicians, plus male and female vocalists and chorus groups, I don't think can ever be duplicated. These days it is hard to find the bands as they perform their now familiar numbers. It was somewhat easier some years ago to find at least one radio station which would carry the sounds, but now even those lone stations are disappearing. The music is still etched on the old recordings, but these also are blowing in the wind. To an old codger like me it's a pitiful shame, but the old must make way for the new, I suppose.

INDUCTED INTO THE ARMY OF THE
UNITED STATES - 1942

I received my "Greeting" letter on December 21, 1942. Uncle Sam gave me his Christmas present! The letter indicated that I had been selected by the Army for training and service and that, therefore, I was to report to the Local Draft Board at 5:45 AM on the last day of the year. Transportation to the induction station at Grand Central Palace, 485 Lexington Ave., NYC would be provided.

At the induction station, we received a thorough physical examination. As I (and most others) passed the exam, we were, with our right hands in the air, forthwith sworn into the Army, to be released from active duty for a week and to report to the Reception Center at Fort Dix, NJ seven days later.

The Local Draft Board informed us that on January 7, 1943 we would report to them, where transportation to Fort Dix would be provided. At Fort Dix I was classified into the Army Signal Corps. Don't ask me why. Maybe they figured I'd make a good messenger or maybe my General Academic High School had an influence. At any rate that was it. The rest was barracks living until later in England, tent living until Reims and Chalons-Sur-Marne in France, and back in the barracks again in Munchen-Gladback and Munich, Germany. Two years, 10 months and 14 days later I was back in my own "barracks" at 30 Cooper Street, NY - home.

WORKED IN SERVICE WITH AUTHOR DASHIELL HAMMETT, SEA GIRT, NJ - 1943

Received my basic training in Sea Girt, NJ. Sea Girt is hard by the Atlantic coast and in February, warmth was not its strong point.

Of course, we lived in barracks - long rows of cots each of which has to be made up stiff as a marble slab, foot lockers, inspections, "gigs", barracks floor scrubbings called "GI parties", up in the dark to the sergeant yelling "drop your cocks and grab your socks", a loudspeaker blaring a John Philip Sousa march for a formation in the cold and wind, calisthenics, good food and plenty of it in thick white china plates and cups, no leisure time, no place to sit and read, latrines loaded with GI's, KP (Kitchen Police), the "Sea Girt Hack" (cough) so bad that tent canvases had to be put up on cots to reduce virus contagion between neighbors, rifle (Enfield) target shooting, and marching, marching, marching -- atten-HUT, forward-HAR, left and right flank, column left and right, left and right oblique, halt, left and right turn, about face, dress right, at ease -- and so it went.

Eventually, I "graduated" and went to Signal Corps message center training at Camp Wood, NJ. We had to walk with full backpack 18 miles between basic training at Camp Edison in Sea Girt to Camp Wood in Eatontown. It took about 10-12 hours. I made it but it sure felt great to finish.

Part of the training calls for running a mock message center. Sitting there writing up these mock messages is a gray-haired, mild mannered guy. He signs them "S. D. Hammett, Cpl". I find out later the guy is Dashiell Hammett - the author! I keep his signature.

Maybe 40 years later, I inquired at an autograph purchasing concern if it were worth anything. They indicated they would pay $50 if it were authentic. They sent me a check when I sent it to them. Too bad I didn't talk much with Mr. Hammett at the time. I just loved his "Thin Man" series.

RODE ACROSS USA IN PULLMAN CAR - NJ TO NV - 1943

After interminable clothing checks, physical exams, paper scrutiny and other red tape, we went by truck to Red Bank, NJ with our loaded barracks bags. We boarded a train for Jersey City, NJ. We (9 guys in our group) got settled in our Pullman Cars and told we wouldn't be changing trains until we reached our final destination - Reno, NV. This was sweet news since those fat barracks bags were heavy, and unwieldy to boot. Surprisingly, we were off in 5 or 10 minutes. They must have been waiting for us!

Since I've never traveled by Pullman before, the accommodations knocked me for a loop; private rooms (although three to a room), upholstered seats convertible into berths, fold-up wash basin, hot water, drinking water, paper cups, 3-speed electric fan, heat control, individual reading lights in berths and last but not least, a private toilet that, with the cover down, looks like an ordinary seat. After going through five months of Signal basic and message center training, where the need for privacy is ripped out of every soldier but good, this was really impressive.

We traveled by B & O tracks south to Washington, DC via Philadelphia, up to Pittsburgh and then Chicago. I slept from before DC to Pittsburgh, but later we passed through McKeesport, PA, Akron, OH and Gary, IN among other places. As for chow, we were previously given 10 bucks a meal and we ate in the dining car. The service was great, but the portions were comparatively small and the food was expensive. We were used to eating army style.

At Chicago, we had four hours before we would have to be back to our Pullman roomettes. Chicago's taxi drivers impressed me with their hustle. And me from New York! At 11:00 PM we were back in our train, this time part of the Union Pacific system, and went through Omaha, NB, Cheyenne, WY, Ogden, UT and, finally, Reno in Nevada.

This country sure is huge. You don't appreciate it until you take a trip like this. We saw a lot of flooded land near the Mississippi, although I missed the old "father of waters" itself. Snap judgments; Iowa - immense farms but dull to look at from a train; Nebraska - smaller farms and more hills and scenery; Wyoming - desolate, treeless and rocky; Utah - not quite as desolate as Wyoming, especially around THE lake which is immense. We traveled over a shallow part of it on a trestle for hours, it seemed like; Nevada - mountains and rocks and mountains and rocks, also sand.

Not counting Chicago, which at its canteen gave us free food, the nicest town we stopped in was North Platte, Nebraska. They brought us baskets of fruit and crackers, magazines and books. Grand Island, Nebraska and Ogden, Utah were also generous to us GI's.

We got into Reno at 4 AM (3 hours late) and were trucked to this Reno Army Air Base some half-hour north of town. The air here is so clear and the sun so sharp, they've warned us about sunburn. Very little rain here, and if you make four right-turns, you'll see four snow-capped mountain ranges. Lot of white, fleecy clouds. Really pretty. I loved this trip!

PARADED AS SOLDIER THROUGH FRESNO, CA - 1943

I don't know exactly why they were having a parade in Fresno, but our Signal Company, the 888th was chosen to represent the army. It had something to do with publicizing the movie "This Is the Army". Music by Irving Berlin, it starred George Murphy and Joan Leslie. All profits went to the Army & Navy Emergency Relief Fund.

It's a lot of waiting around in the hot sun, but a new experience for me to be IN a city parade instead of just watching one. I kind of felt proud and stuck out my chest maybe a little bit further.

We also had a beer party in Roeding Park in Fresno which was a lot of fun. A buddy of mine and I walked away early and went to the nearby zoo. Strange to see a zoo in any other place but the Bronx, NY! It was a smaller one - no tigers, giraffes or elephants, but just about everything else. We enjoyed it.

WATCHED AIR FORCE PLANES TAKEOFF AND LAND, KELLY FIELD, TX - 1943

I'm not sure why, but the name "Kelly Field" had an ambiance of adventure and romance attached to it. I know it did for me in 1943. So when we were stationed in Stinson Field in preparation for shipment overseas, I made a point of visiting nearby Kelly Field.

Transportation between the fields was easy to come by. Just hop a bus. But the great thing was that Kelly Field had a circumnavigation mode of transportation. I grabbed this and remained on it till I had circled the field. It took a half hour or so with the stops, of course.

And if you liked aircraft, this was the ride to take. Although each airfield tended to specialize in the different Air Corps activities (Stinson Field specialized in Air Depot Group activities), Kelly was a general working location. There were many aircraft taking off, landing, taxiing and parked. The trip around the field was an aircraft-lovers delight. I could have stayed on the conveyance for several round-the-field journeys. But one trip was all I had time for.

SAILED ON LINER QUEEN MARY TO EUROPE - 1943

We had an early morning trip by train to Weehauken, NJ across the Hudson River from Manhattan's towers. Weehauken - yes, Aaron Burr shot and mortally wounded Alexander Hamilton here 139 years ago. But I'm not thinking of that now.

Mercifully, we don't have the heavy barracks bags to tote. Just a light backpack. Ferry across the river to 49th Street. Could this mean one of the giant ocean liners which can only tie up at the big piers in Manhattan in the west 40's? It sure can. None other than the Atlantic-crossing record holder - the Queen Mary. Going up the gangplank (along with thousands of other poor Joes), we were handed a pink card which gave us the location of our sleeping quarters.

Every alternate day (there were only 5 days on board); we would sleep in the library (stripped of books, of course, and stacked with bunks maybe five high). On the other day, we would sleep on the Promenade Deck itself, outside the library. The deck was closed off to the elements so I think I liked the deck sleep better - less claustrophobic. We ate in the dining hall below, in shifts, using our mess kits.

On the high seas. The trip was essentially uneventful (thank God for that). I'm palling around with two other guys now, Bascom Knode from Virginia and Pvt Fitzmaurice from Boston. Knode was a cheeky guy - quiet but adventurous. We went everywhere we could on that ship and a few places we shouldn't have. The weather was gray and rough all the way. But the big Lady could handle it easily. I'm prone to fall victim to motion sickness. Even the truck trip to Kings Canyon in California two months earlier had me queasy for awhile. But I was fine on board the Mary. Knode's busy daytime activity program may have had something to do with this.

Although I didn't realize it in the beginning, the ship zig-zagged its way across the Atlantic. Someone said we zigged (or zagged) our way across, every seven minutes. Since German U-boats take more than 7 minutes to sight a ship, launch a torpedo and have it travel to the target (me), the zig-zag course foiled their attempts (unless they got off a real lucky shot). This is also why we traveled alone. A convoy would have only slowed us down. I believe there were about 2500 of us on this little cruise.

UNDERWENT LIVE AMMO OBSTACLE COURSE, WALES - 1944

We got up early and I donned my backpack without help (no mean feat). We started our trip by truck at 0630 and arrived at our destination in Wales at 1700. The weather was good and the Welsh countryside was unexpectedly pretty. Later went to a small nearby town. The people were extremely friendly. Had some beer and walked all over town. Took a civilian bus back to our camp area. I fell in love with the female bus conductor!

We rose early the next morning to go on the machine gun obstacle course. It was very tiring as you have to creep along for quite a distance keeping real low while they fire machine gun bullets over your body. But all went well. Had a sense of accomplishment when it was over.

Went into town in the afternoon on a coal truck. Played snooker (English pool), ate and went to the movies. Bus trip back to camp was fun with the Welsh people. Later, during guard duty, I got this awful cramp in my leg. Guess I did too much today. The next morning a truck convoy took us back to our 877th Signal Company area. One thing I do remember about this trip back to camp was that I had to pee very badly. So it was out the back of the moving truck. Uncouth Yanks!

SAW FLYING 'BUZZ BOMB' SOAR OVER LONDON, FALL & EXPLODE - 1944

I've been to London, England five times. The first three were as a soldier in WW II. The first visit was on a four-hour layover as I traveled in a group from northwestern England to Wiltshire west of London. The second visit was on a 24 hour pass and the third was on a seven day furlough, all in 1944 and '45.

The civilian trips were in 1987 and 1992. The first was on a quest to attain genealogical information on my father's family and ancestors and to see where he lived and worked. The second trip's main focus was to see the daughter of my girlfriend's college chum dance the lead in the ballet "Giselle" at the Royal Opera House.

But I digress. The "buzz bomb" occurrence took place on the occasion of my 24 hour pass to the big city in March of 1944. I recall the event, although I don't recall the circumstances surrounding it. The flying bomb or V-1 had a peculiar and distinctive sound - almost like an outboard motor on a boat. The scary thing was the wait (and silence) between when the engine cut off and the explosion sounded. It must have been about 15 or 20 seconds as I recall. Of course, if it were a distance from you, which this one was, you were out of danger.

LANDED ON OMAHA BEACH, NORMANDY, FRANCE (D+38) - 1944

We crossed the English Channel in a moderate-sized passenger ship, the "Llandley Castle". We boarded the night before. The ship lay at anchor until morning in Portsmouth harbor south of Southampton, England. We slept in hammocks slung between poles. It took some getting used to. The channel crossing was quite pleasant as the weather was great. We passed many convoys of ships in the channel.

As we neared Omaha Beach on the Normandy coast, it looked like a big, high, flat embankment overlooking the strand. This was more than a month after D-Day and the momentous events that occurred there and then. They had since built a pier out into the channel maybe 100 feet or so. The pier would not be strong enough for our ship to tie up to, so we disembarked the "Llandley Castle" by going over the side. We climbed down rope netting, with our backpacks on, into bobbing landing craft or LST's.

After a short trip, we left the LST which was now tied up at the pier ready to cruise back and pick up some more GI's. We walked the short distance on the pier to the beach. Then it was over the beach to a path going up the face of the steep sloping embankment. The path ascended at an angle - sort of a switchback path - so that the hill was not overly steep to walk up. Finally we got to the top of the overlooking embankment.

We hiked through some fields to get cover where we chowed down with our K Rations (a meal on-the-go). Some French people were nearby working or watching. They seemed very friendly - we hadn't worn out our welcome yet.

After a short break, we resumed our hike further inland where we could get under the cover of thicker bushes and trees. The front, by the way, was some 20 miles to the southwest near St. Lo at this time. The cover surrounded a field and constituted the famed "hedgerows" of Normandy. The fields themselves were apple orchards. Since this was July, the apples were not ripe as yet. I'm not sure what they did with the apple crop, but one thing they <u>did</u> do was to make Calvados, the potent Normandy cognac.

And so passed July 14th, 1944 - Bastille Day in France. We snoozed that evening in our pup-tents under the bushes with our recently dug foxholes nearby.

VOTED FOR FDR BY ABSENTEE BALLOT, FRANCE - 1944

My 21st birthday was in June of 1944 making me eligible to vote for president. In early October while in Reims, France, I received my absentee ballot from New York State. Of course, I had previously applied for it. So, four months after becoming eligible, I made my decision on a paper ballot - Franklin Delano Roosevelt for an unprecedented fourth term. I sent the ballot to the States by US Mail.

Between 1944 and 2008 (as I write this), there have been 16 presidential elections. If I make it to November 4th and vote in this year's election, it will be my 17th straight presidential vote.

There have been 55 presidential elections in the history of our country. The year 2008 will make it 56. If I vote in November, 2008, it will be my 17th. In other words, I've voted in 30.4% of the country's presidential elections or almost a third! Doesn't quite seem possible. Furthermore, if I make my 20th presidential election in 2020, not too likely (I'd be 97), I will have voted in more than a third of USA's presidential elections.

Of course, FDR won in 1944 (don't change horses in midstream). So, I began my presidential voting history with an agreement with the majority of Americans.

TOURED CHAMPAGNE CELLAR IN REIMS, FRANCE - 1945

As a member of the Army Signal Corps attached to the Ninth Tactical Air Force in WW II, we were stationed in Reims, France for seven months. Reims is the largest city in the Champagne Region.

We had much to do tending to the communication needs of our advanced air depot group. Naturally, we got into town often. Maybe the two most important tourist spots in the area were the Reims Cathedral and the champagne wine cellars.

The magnificent cathedral, begun in the thirteenth century, was the location for the coronation of most French kings. The wonder of its facade can only be surpassed by the awe of its vast and magnificent interior.

As to the champagne cellars, we visited the Pommery & Greno establishment. They stored their wine in an old Roman mine which maintained a constant 55 degree temperature.

According to our Army booklet, it is not known exactly when the manufacture of champagne was first begun, but it is estimated that it must have been towards the end of the 17th Century. At that time, most of the famous vineyards belonged to monasteries. One monk of the Hautvillers Order had a particular flair for blending the different kinds of grapes, and also found that by substituting corks for the customary oiled hemp stoppers, the wine retained its sparkle. The fame of this new wine soon spread and it was not long before it was found on all the royal tables.

It was not found at our tables in the Army mess hall, but in town on pass it flowed quite freely. Also, on the cellar tour, one could obtain more than a few free samples.

In the cellar during the wines aging, the bottles were stored upside down at a 45 degree angle. This allowed any sediment to gravitate toward the neck of the bottle. The bottles were given a twist occasionally to ensure that the sediment was completely at the top of the bottle neck. Then, one day, the bottle necks were frozen; the stoppers removed and out came the sediment with some frozen wine. Thus, champagne wine is not only sparkling but crystal clear. The whole process was educational and tasteful.

At Reims, France Statue of Louis XIV

WORKED AS CRYPTOGRAPHER IN ENGLAND, FRANCE & GERMANY - 1944/45

Being a cryptographer meant encoding and decoding friendly messages. It did not mean breaking down enemy codes.

As a member of the message center where all means of military communication were available, I suppose I was under the watchful eye of the Message Center Chief, Technical Sergeant Shaeffer and the Cryptographic Chief, Staff Sergeant Lynch. Depending on the volume of message traffic, an opening became available in the Code Room and I was selected. I had done some good work in the distribution of military mail which probably accounted for the upward selection. At any rate, this job began while I was in England and continued as the Signal Company moved to France and finally Germany.

The cryptographer's main tool, besides a typewriter, was the M-209 Converter, a cigar box-sized metal box. It had a hand-turnable wheel on the side providing the 26 letters of the alphabet. Each morning, internal lugs in the machine would be changed in accordance with top secret code books. The lugs would change; say a dialed letter "T", to another letter, providing an encoded letter and eventually an encoded message. Decoding would be the same process in reverse - the encoded letter would provide a decoded letter and a message. Later, a floor-standing model with more 'bells and whistles' was used. British codes, used by us occasionally, required the use of codes written up in pamphlets. The code books were locked in combination lock safes and, in addition, the Code Room was always locked.

PASSED BY WINSTON CHURCHILL OUTSIDE HOUSE OF COMMONS - 1945

Two and a half weeks after cessation of hostilities in Europe, my name came up on the roster to get a one-week furlough to London. How good is that!

On May 25th, having gotten my medical and security clearances in order, I'm off on my visit to London to see the Queen. Well, not quite. The plane was the noisy old workhorse, the C-47, no windows for passengers, and bucket seats facing towards the center of the plane. I have a proneness for motion sickness and I, unfortunately, acquiesced.

But this was my first ever plane trip. The thrill of it made the trip a memorable adventure. What a great way to travel a distance! In London, I did a lot of walking and looking. Later, I met a "Piccadilly Commando". We struck a mutually satisfactory deal. I know it was for me and I'm sure it must have been for her. Had a great time. Later, checked out some of the speakers in Hyde Park. Very interesting.

Took a tour of the town in a London cab. I had a good man as a guide. These cabs are great. Later, saw "The Three Caballeros" a Disney movie with Sterling Holloway and still later, the play "While Parents Sleep". The latter, a comedy, was at the Whitehall Theatre on Trafalgar Square and starred Phyllis Dixey. John Nicolson was in the play also. The small, wartime theatre program cost sixpence. I wasn't particularly enamored with the production.

I had one chore to perform on my furlough. I had to deliver some money to a GI by the name of Kornbau who was in a hospital in Romford where I had been about a year ago. I didn't make any connections with my former Romford acquaintances, so it was back to London and more walking around. Then, some relaxation at the American Red Cross (ARC) Club.

The London ARC Club, according to a weekly newsletter "London ARC Light", May 19, 1945, is composed of 18 ARC Clubs in Greater London - one for service women, one for women officers, five for (male) officers and eleven for us regular GI Joes. They run programs and have events at all of them on a scheduled basis. They have dances, discussion and instruction sessions, entertainment and social events, sports, music, tours of London and environs, first run movies, and other incidental services, like providing workout rooms, secretarial service, free ticket bureaus and afternoon outings. I availed myself of the London taxi tour, the free theatre ticket service and the tours of the Houses of Parliament and Reuters News Agency. Of course, there were a few other things they didn't list that I found on my own - wink, wink.

Later, I saw Thornton Wilder's "The Skin of Our Teeth" - the history of the world in a comic strip. Vivien Leigh had top billing and the production was directed by someone I had never heard of - Laurence Olivier! Since a lot of it went over my head, I didn't particularly enjoy it, sorry to say.

Up for a tour of the Houses of Parliament on the banks of the Thames. Everything is stone and wood and built to last. The chamber of the House of Commons struck me strange, like a giant, half-opened book with tiers of seats on both halves, the presiding officers and parliamentarians in between at the front end. God, what words have been spoken and listened to here. And the speakers and listeners - the two Pitts, Edmund Burke, Disraeli, Gladstone, Lloyd George, Churchill and so many others.

But, enough culture for one day. Phillis Dixey again, this time in "Peek-A-Boo". Then, in the evening, "Shop at Sly Corner", a thriller in three acts, at the St. Martin's Theatre which I enjoyed very much. Cathleen Nesbitt had a leading role. After the theater, who should I run into but my first-night Commando. It was a long day. The next day, after some writing, went to a News Theatre for an hour, then on a tour of the Reuters News Agency. The place was very busy and interesting. A sample news item transmitted instantly from Scotland:

> "When Mr Churchill was asked by Mr Rhys Davies, Labor, West-Houghton, to give information as to the transfer of vessels of the Royal Navy to the Red Fleet, the Prime Minister said he would defer the answer which would be somewhat lengthy until next week. Mr Rhys Davies reminded the Prime Minister that he had said he did not propose to preside over the liquidation of the British Empire. Mr Churchill indicated that this particular episode was part of the process by which the consolidation of the British Empire was achieved. * * * ".

After some tea and crackers, it was off to see Lindsay and Crouse's "Arsenic and Old Lace" - "a new comedy" at the Strand - which gave its 1000th performance two weeks earlier. I had seen it in New York and preferred the NY version. Later, at one of the hotels, I saw two US Senators, Kilgore and Brewster. Finished another good day listening to the Hyde Park speakers.

Saw Fred Allen in "The Fifth Chair" with Binnie Barnes. It was OK. Then, to that old London standby for visitors, Madame Tussaud's Exhibition (the Wax Museum) with its 435 exhibits including 7 tableaus and 84 Chamber of Horrors exhibits. The figures are amazingly life-like, to be sure. Later, I sauntered around the Piccadilly Circus area and picked up a cute little commando. She certainly wasn't as professional as the other lady. She apologized more than once for living several blocks off the main drag and for my having to walk two or three flights up to her flat (horrors). We had a fine time and she invited me to stay the whole night. I had a mind-set to spend an hour or two, so I left. Big mistake. She was nice and relatively unsophisticated. This was a high point of my furlough in old London town so far.

I loafed around the Westminster area where the Abbey, Parliament and Big Ben are situated and watched the Thames, and things on the Thames, float by. I had an appointment at 3 PM, arranged by the Columbia ARC Club, to meet the Lord Fermoy! The card I carried said, "This will introduce T.5. R. Ward". The tour allowed me (and others) to see parliament in session. But the most lasting memory of this week occurred when I was standing outside the House of Commons when who should walk by at arm's length but Winston Leonard Spencer Churchill himself and, I think, his colleague Ernest Bevin. Winny look so short, so stooped and, it seemed to me, so pink. So much for historical figures. Later, I walked around Piccadilly on a fruitless quest to find my paramour of the night before. "Ships that pass in the night - - - ". Went to bed early.

Up at 9:30. Took the train to Cumberley for the plane trip back to Germany. Waiting for the flight, I gave serious consideration to going back to London and staying there. That was one hell of a town. But, flight time came and I was there. I'm a seasoned air traveler now! No sickness. But my ears hurt this time, I guess with the congestion in my head. So, so sorry the trip was over.

SAW ADOLF HITLER'S BURNED OUT
EAGLES NEST, AUSTRIA - 1945

One day, a dozen or so of us pile into a couple of trucks for a sightseeing trip. We're heading for Berchtesgaden in Germany, about 70 miles to the southeast of Munich and 10 miles south of Salzburg, Austria.

Berchtesgaden is the nearest town to Hitler's vacation spot, "The Eagle's Nest". Actually, the "Nest" requires a ten minute walk further up the 6000 foot mountain after alighting from the trucks. The concrete building, overlooking a spectacular view of mountains, valleys, lakes, streams and waterfalls, was largely destroyed by explosives of some kind. Naturally, the view remains.

It's not difficult to imagine the man - the one most directly responsible for disrupting and causing suffering, chaos and death to more than half the world's population - and his girlfriend, Eva Braun, having a very relaxing time at this beautiful aerie when it was in functioning order.

RECEIVED HONORABLE DISCHARGE
FROM MILITARY SERVICE - 1945

November 14th - the big one - discharge day. Oh, how I waited for this grand day. We were in the Separation Center, Ft. Dix, NJ where I went into active duty 1045 days ago. Again with the clothing checks, payroll signing, showdown inspections, pay distributions and talks. But, finally, the paper we had waited for - the Honorable Discharge.

"This is to certify that" I am honorably discharged from military service. The certificate also indicates that it is awarded as a testimonial of honest and faithful service to the United States of America. And on the reverse, it gives credit for assisting in four battles and campaigns, confirms a rating for two medals and an accounting of my monetary entitlements - mustering out pay, soldier deposit, travel pay from Ft. Dix to NYC ($3.95) and final military pay. The whole thing amounted to $506.82. $200 more was coming of the spaced-out mustering out pay.

And then, it was head for the trains, back to Pennsylvania Station in New York, the "A" (subway) train to 207th Street in Manhattan and the walk home to family and pets with a lot of hugging and kissing, although we are not normally a very demonstrative family. Oh, the bed felt good that night.

Adjustment to civilian life was on the horizon. It was made easier by the "GI Bill of Rights" which bankrolled a four year university education at New York University leading to a Bachelor of Arts degree in psychology.

Author Soon After Army Discharge>>

CAMPED OUT WITH BROTHER BILL FOR FIVE DAYS, LAKE TIORATI, BEAR MOUNTAIN, NY - 1947

I'm not sure how it started, but Bill and I would go on short adventures here and there. They gradually got longer. Bill somehow obtained a used 1938 Chevrolet. He was good at getting what he wanted. He got a bicycle when he was younger. I never had one when I was a kid. Of course, I had <u>my</u> younger days during the Great Depression. That put a damper on acquisition of material goods as a kid. Bill, on the other hand, grew up during WW II time and after. The Depression was gone then - but not forgotten.

At any rate, we started to take the Chevy to more distant campsites. One time we went almost to the eastern tip of Long Island at Montauk Point for one of our camping trips - to Hither Hills State Park. This park was more than 100 miles east of NYC where we lived. The park was right on the Atlantic coast although the camp site was somewhat inland. It was a beautiful place to swim and surf and watch the waves and shore birds. As we watched the waves, we thought every seventh wave was bigger than the others!

One day we got the inspiration to camp in Bear Mountain State Park. The state of New York is blessed with many parks with campsites. About 30 miles up the Hudson River from the city, it had several camp sites. We chose Lake Tiorati.

It was fun setting up the tent, arranging the fire site for cooking, going to the lake for our daily swim or hike or rowboat trip, cooking the meals and getting a good night's sleep in the tent. On our rowboat adventures, we'd jump off the boat in the middle of the lake and swim around just for the fun of it. Of course, the car allowed for an easier time of it transporting the camping paraphernalia to and fro. When Bill's war came along in the early 50's (Korea), I inherited the Chevy. I took it down to Washington, DC where I had gotten a job with the Census Bureau. I eventually traded the old oil-burner in for a used 1950 Ford.

SHOVELED SNOW FOR NYC
AFTER BLIZZARD OF '47 - 1948

The Blizzard of '47 struck NYC on the day after Christmas. Needless to say it paralyzed the city. As I recall, we got three inches more than two feet of snow. It killed 55 people. The only disruption to our family, as I remember it, were no milk deliveries for several days. In those days milk was delivered to your doorstep in time for breakfast, even if you lived in a five story walk-up apartment house like we did. The milkman with his horse and wagon did the job although I don't remember exactly when this practice ceased.

But the snowstorm brought the city to a standstill. The city was in trouble. First, the white stuff had to be shoved to the side in long rows. Then, bigger equipment could consolidate the rows into gigantic hills of snow. Luckily the presence of parked automobiles was not as big a problem as it is today. Finally, the dirty snow mountains (which gave the kids a whole lot of fun by playing "fort" on them) had to be loaded into trucks and carted to the river to be dumped.

The city put out a call for manpower to shovel the darkening precipitation into uncovered sewer manholes. We were told to go to various sites and directed to follow orders on snow removal procedures. This was about two or three weeks after the December 26th blizzard.

Fire hoses did the final cleanup by slushing the stuff down the sewer. I remember though when hard freezes came, and left the streets worse off than they were before. In this eventuality, the only viable solution was to wait for a spell of above freezing weather. Then, the leftover ice could be hastened down the drains with more manpower and water hoses. Of course, we got paid for this manual labor - enough to make it worthwhile but not enough to make you rich. But eventually spring came and the Blizzard of '47 was relegated to memory. Everyone was happy to reclaim their streets and have the storm behind them.

TALKED WITH REP. JACOB JAVITS (R-NY) IN HOUSE CORRIDOR, DC - 1948

It was my junior year at New York University. It was also an election year. On top of that, it was the first time in 20 years that Franklin D. Roosevelt was not running for president. He died, of course, three years earlier.

Being a veteran, I had also joined the American Veterans Committee in my young college days. This organization was somewhat more political than either the American Legion or the Veterans of Foreign Wars. The AVC also had less conservative positions than the Legion or the VFW.

Putting these events together, I became an uncharacteristically strong political activist. I jumped at the chance to take a trip to Washington, DC with a group of other students of a similar vein. We went by train to the District and made sure that we didn't stay or eat at any Jim Crow facility, of which there were a few in post WW II Washington, DC. The main focus of the trip, however, was to talk with our elected representatives in Congress about our political concerns.

My representative from the 21st Congressional District (since changed) in New York was Jacob K. Javits. He represented the northern part of Manhattan and a good bit of The Bronx. Albeit a Republican, he had many liberal views regarding labor and race relations. Eight years later in 1956, he defeated Robert F. Wagner, Jr. in a hotly contested race for Senator Herbert Lehman's old senate seat. Javits, like Lehman before him, was the only Jewish member of the US Senate.

But in 1948, we met the representative in the House corridor in the US Capitol Building. It was a daunting experience for me. I don't remember exactly what we talked about, but it was probably about jobs creation and race relations. Later that year, I voted in my second presidential election. Although I thought President Truman had done a good job, my youthful zeal required that I vote for one of the third party candidates. There were two. One was Strom Thurmond, the States Rights candidate and the other was Henry Wallace, the former Secretary of Agriculture. Of course, Wallace got my vote. In other words, Harry S. Truman pulled the upset of the century with no help from me!

GRADUATED WITH BA DEGREE (PSYCHOLOGY) FROM NEW YORK UNIVERSITY - 1949

As stated before (Graduation from George Washington High School - 1941), I had missed my high school graduation mainly because of a mysterious illness I'd somehow contracted. But eight years later, after working for two years in downtown Manhattan, spending three years in the army (two overseas) and taking three and a half years to soak up a college knowledge, it finally came time for me to graduate from the university. Had my picture and small write-up in the yearbook, completed all my scholastic requirements and everything was set to go. This would have been a fancy, super-duper graduation on the grounds of the beautiful Bronx campus at University Heights overlooking the Harlem River. (High above the Harlem's waters!).

But for some reason, I didn't attend. No excuse that I can remember, I just didn't go. Looking back on it 59 years later I believe it was my old timidity rearing its ugly head. Also, the pomp and circumstance of a grand graduation just didn't seem so important to me after the army years, traversing the USA twice and spending a couple of years in Europe. I can't recall asking my parents if they wanted to go or the rest of my family. I don't see why they would not have considered it.

So, one of my life's milestones just slip by without a ripple. As I look back on it, of course, I wish I had gone, if only for the experience. Needless to say, I nevertheless received the important document, the diploma, which turned my life around from shipping clerk in a typewriter repair company to a civil service employee in the Federal Government. But, I didn't participate in the graduation and that's that.

DELIVERED MAIL FOR POST OFFICE - 1949

It takes awhile to marry up your education with your career. I wanted to get into personnel activities, but it doesn't happen overnight. I first opted to obtain a post office job as my near term objective, then, long term, I would take a civil service test to gain entry into the federal government. As a child of the Great Depression, a federal retirement pension appealed to me quite a bit.

For the US Postal Service (it was a part of the federal government in those days), I signed up to deliver special delivery mail in Manhattan. It was fairly satisfying employment. I knew midtown quite well having delivered typewriter parts in mid and lower Manhattan in 1942.

We had a fine opportunity to meet lots of pretty secretaries when delivering the mail and getting signatures. The work combined outdoor and indoor activities which suited me just fine. One thing the job had in abundance - elevator riding. Virtually every special delivery recipient did business high in a tall building or skyscraper. I used Mr. Otis' invention very often. But I loved the trips through midtown Manhattan. I felt I was a part of something big and important.

WORKED ON MAIDEN LANE, DOWNTOWN MANHATTAN - 1949

On my next job, I hooked up with an insurance firm. Actually it was a group of insurance companies. This time it was all indoor work, sitting at a desk, surrounded by other people sitting at their desks. At the desk in back of me was a young lady, Dolores Biancomano by name. We did pretty much the same thing - keep track of the vital statistics of each of our member companies.

As I look back on those days, it seemed like Dolores was trying to make it easy for me to get to know her better. But I was too shy or too dumb to succumb to her mild advancements. I remember one time we had to go together down into the isolated records storage area. I had a golden opportunity to get physically close to her, but, alas, failed to do so. We did have a date one time to meet at the Central Park Lake which was frozen for ice-skating, but I have no recollection of how events turned out.

The most memorable part of this job, however, was the street location - downtown Manhattan, four short blocks north and parallel to Wall Street - Maiden Lane. According to computer research, Maiden Lane received its name because, in the old Dutch days in the 1600's, maidens would leave the confines of the wall (hence Wall Street) and walk up to where a stream flowed that emptied into the East River to the east. They would wash clothes in the stream and the path they used became - yes, indeed - Maiden Lane. Of course, the stream has long since been put underground, but the maidens are still there. But, there is no such thing as clothes washing, just tall buildings, cement sidewalks and asphalt streets. Pity.

Anyhow, I worked on Maiden Lane without washing clothes.

ENTERED FEDERAL CIVIL SERVICE EMPLOYMENT WITH CENSUS BUREAU, MD - 1950
ASSISTED IN 1950 US DECENNIAL CENSUS, WASHINGTON, DC

I passed the civil service test with a high grade. In those days relatively soon after years of schooling, taking tests is an easy proposition, provided you know your subject. You may look forward to the task with a degree of apprehension, but having taken tests for years, it comes with little difficulty.

After several months I received word from the Census Bureau, a part of the Commerce Department, that an opening for me was available. I answered in the affirmative. I had minored in college in statistics and thought this was a good opportunity.

The Bureau was located in its own new building several miles to the southeast of the District of Columbia in a place called Suitland, MD. I took public transportation east on famed Pennsylvania Avenue to get there. When I first arrived in DC I stayed at the YMCA downtown. I soon moved to a rooming house on East Capitol Street near Pennsylvania Avenue in Southeast, DC.

My first assignment after orientation involved desk work where I had to improve and simplify wherever I could the instructions provided to census-takers in the 1950 Census. My boss was a Jewish guy from New York, so we got along fine. Also at the desk next to me was an African/American female, also from New York City and also an attendee of NYU. She later graduated from the University of California at Berkeley. Her field was economics. We got to be close friends as the weeks went by.

Several months later, I was assigned as a "Contact Coder". The position was located in a "Tempo Building" on the Reflecting Pool in Washington, DC. This is where the census forms, called schedules, were transformed from census-takers handwriting to IBM cards for later machine manipulation. I led a team of half a dozen colleagues to answer the questions of the clerks (mostly women) whose job it was to punch in the data. When an entry was missing, garbled or made no sense, we were called upon to decide what the proper entry should be. It was an interesting assignment.

But soon enough, the last of the schedules was completed - compilation of the 1950 Census would just about be history. I searched around for other federal employment.

MET LIFE COMPANION, THELMA MARTIN, FELLOW NY'ER AND NYU'ER, AT CENSUS - 1951

As mentioned, at my first government job at the Census Bureau, next to me was an African/ American female named Thelma Martin. We had a lot in common. She was also from NYC and also studied at NYU. She completed her master's degree at California, Berkeley, however.

I thought I loved NY to an excessive degree - it was nothing compared to Thelma. It was her favorite subject. She grew up in her teenage years in the Bronx somewhat near The Bronx Zoo on Paulding Avenue. She was born on 79th Street in Manhattan. Her father worked for the Frick's. He made his money in steel in Pittsburgh. The Frick's, millionaires in their day, had a mansion on 72nd Street, I believe. Thelma's father worked as a manservant in that household. The mansion, years later, became an art museum -- open to this day.

But as to our (Thelma's and mine) relationship outside the workplace, it started very slowly. We lost touch with each other as we were given other Census assignments. But we did use the phone as we lived in different parts of the District of Columbia. One day, as I recall, she called me and we talked for 30 or 40 minutes. The conversations were somewhat one-sided as she was a great talker and I at that time, quite the opposite. Once, as she was talking, I left the phone to do some chore for perhaps two or three minutes and when I picked up the receiver again she was still talking!

But she had a tremendous disposition, loved life, people and travel (besides NYC). We soon grew more fond of each other and had a close relationship for 40 years, although we had separate apartments (mail drops) in the same apartment house. We both eventually left the Census Bureau, she going to the Health and Human Services Department and I to the Army Department. She was my companion on no less than six total solar and one annular (ring) eclipse trips ranging from Virginia, Montana, Mexico, Uruguay, India and a Far East cruise on 'The Golden Odyssey'. I used to say about her that she "collected people". She loved that phrase.

However, she was older than me and one awful day in DC, she died of a heart attack. Of course, I missed her terribly, but life goes on. In fact, my life had a second flowering because of Thelma, as you will find out on subsequent pages.

PLAYED 'SWEET SUE' ON GUITAR, STUDENT'S CONCERT, DC - 1952

When I first came to Washington, DC to work at the Census Bureau, I stayed at the YMCA. Eventually, I opted for a rental room, obtained through the Bureau, complete with roommate - a fellow Census worker from South Carolina by name Copeland Granger. We got along OK even though he was a "Rebel" and I, a "Yankee". I think we both learned something from the experience.

But, I had time on my hands after work. I decided to take lessons on playing the guitar. I had a good instructor I thought. He was a Latino. Of course, he taught me how to tune the instrument, how to finger the strings and frets, how to position for chords and how to read notes from sheet music. I had always been musically inclined.

Eventually, the instructor set up a concert of his students. All of the other students were school kids, maybe 12 to 18 years of age. Here I was, a WW II vet pushing 30! I did feel self-conscious. But with the urging of the instructor, I joined the concert.

The number I had down fairly well was "Sweet Sue". I felt I had done a decent job on the tune and no one seemed to disagree. I must say it was fun once it was over. One gets a certain feeling of confidence on being the center of attraction for a brief time. I had even bought my own instrument, no doubt with the instructor's assistance.

But, alas, practice makes perfect. I was reluctant to do the homework after a day spent at the Bureau. Also, I thought it would not help my roommate on his time off. So, after the guitar lessons were over my guitar playing time dwindled and finally disappeared altogether. Too bad. After many years passed, I priced the guitar at a local dealer. He pointed out several flaws in the instrument, caused by idle years in the closet, rendering it useless to anyone but myself. Thus, I never became another Les Paul.

Several months after the student concert, the instructor invited me to a local bar with a small dance floor. He was in a small band and invited me to take a turn supplying the beat on the drums. I did for about five minutes - I'll stick to the guitar.

OBSERVED REVERSING RAPIDS (SAINT JOHN) & TIDAL BORE (MONCTON), NB, CANADA - 1952

On my vacation from work, I decided to motor through New England and into New Brunswick, Canada. I asked my dad and sister if they'd like to accompany me and they jumped at the chance. I had bought by then a used 1950 Ford, so that was our mode of travel.

When my father came over from his native England in 1910, he arrived in Halifax, Nova Scotia. He wound up in Toronto, Ontario for six years before immigrating to the USA. He married my mom in 1921 in NYC.

But we took off through New England and four or five days later we approached Saint John, New Brunswick on a drizzly day. I wheeled the car into an open area beside some other cars for no particular reason save to stretch our legs. Upon alighting from the car, we were amazed to discover we were on the top and near the edge of a vertical cliff some 200 feet above a black, vicious-looking river, whose waters were streaked with swift moving foam lines and riddled with hundreds of whirlpools and eddies of differing dimensions.

The river was the Saint John River. But Saint John was near the Bay of Fundy, famous the world over as the home of thirty foot tides. So, the river would make its way to the bay in a normal fashion during a lower tide and during high tide, the bay water would wend its way back up the river - The Reversing Rapids! There was a restaurant nearby from which you could sit and eat or drink and watch the rapids. We did so at the time of the changing of the river's direction, which would take a matter of 15 minutes to a half hour. It was intensely interesting to me to watch the waters reverse, surely a non-ordinary event.

A day or two later we arrived in Moncton also in N.B. The weather was much better with a bright sun soon to set. We stopped at a small park overlooking the river - this time the Pettitcodiac River. The park was specially located to view the Tidal Bore, on a high bluff overlooking a big bend in the river. A big iron clock had been emplaced in the park indicating the time of the next bore.

The scene before us was engrossing. It was a vast brown mud plain with the tiny river splitting the plain down the middle, before bending downstream to the right. Gulls and other shore birds were picking the sandy mud plain for sustenance.

But the time of the bore approached. People had gathered along the bluffs edge to witness the bore. Slowly, around the bend to our left, a tan wave of water was rolling upstream to our right. It took maybe five minutes to round the bend, inundating the mud plain as it advanced. The birds had to scatter as the Tidal Bore overtook them. With the slowly setting sun at our backs, our shoreline shadows could be seen wriggling eerily in the Pettitcodiac. When we left, the vast mud plain had been transformed into a vast estuary of tan water. We were so happy and thrilled to have witnessed the Tidal Bore of Moncton, NB, Canada, but we had other sights to see.

CLIMBED TALLEST PEAK IN WEST VIRGINIA, SPRUCE KNOB - 1953

I once had a grandiose plan to climb the tallest peaks in each of the nearby states. I love high places. Of course, coming from NYC, I've been to the top of the Empire State Building, 86 stories above Manhattan's streets. There is a tower which rises another 16 stories, but it's not open to the public. It's a gratifying experience, particularly since one is out in the open up there on the building. The building was erected when I was 7 or 8 years old and I remember its construction.

Other NY high places I've been to include Rockefeller Center and the International Trade Center before it was destroyed by Osama Bin Laden and his band of 'angry' men on 9/11/01.

But, back to the tallest peaks. Since I resided in Washington, DC at the time, I decided to start off in West Virginia, probably because of something I read. The name of the highest peak there is Spruce Knob.

I recall driving there and approaching the peak relatively closely in my car. But then it was time to get out and walk - more or less vertically. Eventually, I reached the top and, of course, was rewarded with beautiful vistas in all 360 degrees of the compass. I had the peak all to myself - not another soul was in sight. I enjoyed the experience so much, but the time came when I had to retrace my path back to the car, back to civilization, back home to DC.

On other 'peak' trips, I visited North Carolina's tallest - Mt. Mitchell. However, no foot climbing was necessary there. The car could be parked near the peak. Then there was New Hampshire's Mt. Washington, not only NH's tallest peak, but the tallest peak on the US northeastern seaboard. I'll have the story of this trip in a later description of a non-ordinary event. But, alas, that was the final tallest peak expedition. Other priorities, you know.

I did climb Virginia's "Old Rag" as it's called. This required a rather strenuous maybe 1/2 hour climb. But, indeed it was worth it. I had my packed lunch up there while enjoying the view. My sense of accomplishment was shattered, however, when some guy met me up there. He told me that he had jogged up the mountain! Well, I was still pleased with myself for my trip from home to the top of "Old Rag" (and back).

VISITED WW II ARMY BUDDY, JACK LAMPENFELD & HIS FAMILY, ON CAR TRIP TO PITTSBURGH, PA. - 1953

I had a lot of nerve in my younger days. After spending a few days with my family in NYC, I decided to drive back to my room in Washington, DC by way of Pittsburgh and drop in on my old army buddy from WW II, Jack Lampenfeld. We were together working in the same message center from late 1943 through mid 1945.

I never wrote him except for one postal card soon after the war had ended and we had gone our separate ways. So eight years later I showed up on his doorstep in Pittsburgh. He had a wife and two kids and all five of us seemed happy to meet. He was driving a taxi while going to school in the evening. He was soft spoken, intelligent, unpretentious and fun-loving. We had gotten along good in Europe.

In the afternoon, he and his wife and kids took me on a small sightseeing tour of the town. We talked about Pittsburgh's great football teams, both university and professional. He was sure the teams would be back to their earlier glory days. In the evening we had a fine dinner at his place and later on they put me up in their big guest bedroom. After a long day, I was tired and slept soundly.

After all Jack and I had been through in England, France and Germany - our trip to Paris, our walks through the German countryside trying to hook up with two buxom milk maidens, our off- duty activity of pumping iron and playing table tennis (he was an expert at the game) - it was a great visit, as his two kids kicked up a fuss in the living room that evening. I left the next morning for DC and home, driving over mountainous and scenic roads. Since the trip started in NYC with my visit to the United Nations Headquarters in Manhattan, the whole excursion was a real fine diversion from the work-a-day world of government employment to which I was soon to return.

As a postscript, about 35 years later, I called Lamp on the phone, but his wife answered. I wanted to talk with my old buddy, but Mrs. Lampenfeld told me he wouldn't remember me or comprehend. She told me he had Alzheimer's Disease. That was a shocker. So sorry to get that news.

With Army Buddy Jack Lampenfeld, Paris

WAS BEST MAN AT MY BROTHER BILL'S WEDDING TO JEAN HOCK - 1954

My brother (his war was in Korea) wasted no time in finding and wooing the prettiest girl in NYC. And Jean Hock was smart also. I was working in Washington during this time so I was unaware that their situation was getting serious. But obviously it was - they've been married now for 54 years and counting. Bill was a lineman in the army, working on erecting telephone networks in Korea.

But I learned one day that I was to be Best Man at his wedding. They were married in a small and pretty Lutheran Church in our neighborhood in uptown Manhattan, known as Inwood. I scarcely remember details of that day. I do remember being alone with him in a small room before the ceremony. I was 31 and he was 24 so I did feel as if I were his protector and guardian, like the time I confronted a mother whose kid ran off with Bill's bicycle, maybe seven years earlier.

I don't remember the wedding itself much. I do remember more of the reception later where all of the families were gathered. I remember being embarrassed when I had to toast the newlyweds. No one told me and I didn't know I had to do it. The toast was quite simple - maybe "Here's to the bride and groom". Forty three years later when I married and he was Best Man at our wedding, he said the same thing!

But, the reception eventually came to an end, the couple went on their honeymoon, the families dispersed, and the day - August 28, 1954 came to an end. I probably returned to Washington the next day to go back to work.

STOOD AT DIAMOND SHOALS POINT, CAPE HATTERAS, NC - 1956

Well, where will I go on this year's summer vacation? In the seven previous years, I'd been to Montauk Point, NY, (camping with brother Bill), Ausable Chasm, NY, with dad, New Brunswick/ Nova Scotia with dad and sister Marian, Pittsburgh, PA, Ontario, Canada, on my own to be disappointed by a clouded out total solar eclipse and the New Jersey shore from Asbury Park to Cape May. This year I opted for North Carolina - from the outer banks to the Great Smoky Mountains - again on my own.

I was impressed with the Nags Head region of the Banks. The Wright Brothers picked a great site to make history with their first heavier-than-air airplane flight. The museum was well worth the side trip. Kill Devil Hills, Jockey's Ridge, Roanoke Island where the summer epic play is performed - all in this area. And the swimming was nonpareil, all along the coast.

But I received my biggest thrill in the Cape Hatteras area. The famed lighthouse, when it was closer to the Atlantic, was a genuine point of interest. It filled the bill with my love of high places. The climb up was fun.

But later or maybe the next day I walked along the beach from the lighthouse south to the cape itself, maybe a 20/30 minute walk. At the very tip of the cape the Atlantic waves come in from the east and on the other side of the cape the waters undulate in from the south. When the two wave patterns cross at a right angle, a "diamond" is formed - hence Diamond Shoals Point. Further out in the water, it's the waves that cross each other, but closer to shore, succeeding wavelets cross each other to form the "diamonds". It's an interesting phenomenon to have your bare feet caressed by the sparkling watery gems.

The rest of the Carolina trip took in Chapel Hill and their planetarium, Mount Mitchell, Fontana Dam, the Cherokee villages and, high-tailing it for home, the Blue Ridge Parkway. At this time, of course, little did I realize that in 41 years I would become an honest-to-goodness "Tarheel" myself. My new wife and I would make New Bern, NC our home.

As fine as this trip was, it should not have been made. My mom couldn't survive the cancer she had. I was in Washington, of course, when I started the journey and I was incommunicado during the week. My loving and much loved mom was dead and buried when I called home after the trip. Such a sad report.

BOUGHT FIRST OF FOUR VOLKSWAGEN "BEETLES" WHICH WERE USED FOR OVER FORTY YEARS - 1956

Why did I buy my first VW "beetle" back in 1956? I can think of a number of reasons. First, it was relatively cheap - if I'm not mistaken it cost less than $2000. Second, it was miserly with gasoline. When I kept track of my miles per gallon, which I did very regularly, I could easily attain 30 MPG and more on the highway. Third, Consumer Reports Magazine, to which I was a subscriber for many years, gave the vehicle high marks for reliability and economy. Fourth, I didn't see the point in a car changing its styling every year whether it needed to or not! And fifth, being single at the time, me and my girlfriend didn't need a lot of extra room in the car - no family.

Perhaps a sixth reason might be that I myself am economical. I couldn't see paying a lot of money for a vehicle to get you from point A to point B. In other words, I was interested in transportation and not in having an extension of my personality or in making an impression on the neighbors.

However, that 1956 VW had a feature which was changed by 1960 when I bought my second beetle. For simplicity's sake, the '56 model had no fuel gauge. If you ran out of fuel you would turn a lever beneath the dashboard and tap into an emergency supply of gasoline which would get you to the next gas station. I was happy when they changed that feature in the '60 model. I didn't like sputtering to a stop in traffic and ducking under the dashboard to give the lever a quarter turn for more gas. I much preferred to keep track of my miles driven and anticipate the need for more gas before the sputter.

But over the forty years that I had four VW beetles, I was completely satisfied. When I finally slipped out of the beetle mode, it was to another VW model - the Golf. It was roomier, had four doors, had a lower interior noise level and, in short, was more of a "regular" vehicle. Age had made me crave more comfort, I suppose.

First of Four VW 'Beetles'

CROSSED STRAITS OF MACKINAC, MICHIGAN BY FERRY - 1957 WATCHED SHIPS TRAVERSE LOCKS, SAULT STE. MARIE, MI/CAN.

This year we decided to take my summer vacation trip to Michigan. So my father and I took off in my VW to the land of automobiles, lake front vistas, northern climes and cherries.

Using the Pennsylvania Turnpike, we continued on Interstate Highway 80 through Ohio and entered Michigan at the southeast corner. Soon we were in the Detroit environs. The next day, we took in the amazingly large Ford River Rouge Plant in Dearborn. We toured the monstrous plant and witnessed the assembly of many cars while we there. They had their own steel mill and manufactured most all other parts that makeup a modern automobile. We were impressed.

But then we continued north passed the "thumb" of Michigan, stopping at various restaurants and overlooks to view the inland sea called Lake Huron to the east of the state. We finally arrived in the Mackinac area where the upper and lower peninsulas of the state meet.

I remember spending an afternoon on Mackinac Island, sitting on the long porch of the big and venerable hotel, overlooking the Mackinac Straits. I don't remember if we spent the night there. The next day we were headed for the UP as they call it, the Upper Peninsula. Spanning the Straits, between the peninsulas, was this beautiful suspension bridge - the second longest suspension bridge in the country at the time, after the Golden Gate Bridge in California. Although almost completed, the bridge wasn't ready for traffic. We missed the opening by a month or two. We waited in our car to line up to take the ferry to the UP. The ferry trip passed relatively quickly. We were engrossed, however, with the water views of the strait and with scenes of the ocean-going ore boats and freighters passing by.

Still traveling north in the car, we arrived at the town of Sault Ste. Marie and across the Canadian border, the other Sault Ste. Marie! The big deal here was watching lake shipping passing through the locks from Lake Superior to the North Channel and Lake Huron. We spent some time here watching the raising and lowering of ships in the massive locks.

But this was our high water mark. From now on we retraced our tire tracks back to Interstate 80 and NYC, but this time traversing Michigan on its west facing side along Lake Michigan. Dad and I enjoyed this trip. Dad was 71 and I'm glad he got to see more of our country than New York. Soon we were home.

RODE INCLINE RAILWAY UP
MT. WASHINGTON, NH - 1959

The big summer trip this year was to New England. Dad and I hopped in the VW and took off one day toward Cape Cod. We passed Newport, Rhode Island and just happened to get there when the famous annual Newport Jazz Festival was about to commence. We were approached by some friendly "hippies" who assumed we were attending the festivities, which we weren't. We did see the summertime waterfront mansions of the rich and famous of yesteryear in Newport. They were sumptuous to say the least. I guess at least some of them are now museums.

Further east, we crossed into Massachusetts and up the "hook" of Cape Cod. We reached Truro near where we saw a dead, beached whale on the strand. Then it was back around the "hook" and up through Boston, and then Saugus, where we visited a colonial iron works.

But the focus of the trip was Mt. Washington, the highest point in New Hampshire at 6288 feet, and indeed the highest point on the east coast save for North Carolina's Mt. Mitchell, some 400 feet higher. We could drive a good bit of the way to get to the lower terminus of the mountain's incline railway. The railway is a cog railway so that the driving wheel is geared to mesh with teeth in the center of the track. Of course, this permits the train to climb at a steeper rate than would be otherwise possible.

When we reached the top, we were in snow. We walked to a shelter where a climatological station was situated. They get some of the stiffest winds ever recorded in this area. But, perhaps, it was the journey that was of greater interest than the destination. The drizzly weather at the top made for poor visibility. No mountain-top vistas on this day - the climb to the top on the incline railway was the adventure. Dad and I both thought we had added a milestone in our lives.

WATCHED BULL FIGHTS IN MEXICO CITY, MEX. - 1961

Because my girlfriend Thelma was African/American and I was Caucasian, we both felt reluctant in these early days to travel together too much. So we made our early trips overseas. I suppose we felt that there was less of a stigma in foreign countries to be seen together.

Thelma had gone to Cuba and Haiti some years before on her own. And, of course, I had spent my summer vacations traveling with my dad and sister. But this year, after traveling through Pennsylvania (Gettysburg, the Dutch Country, Pittsburgh) with dad, Thelma and I made our first larger trip by flying to Mexico City and Acapulco.

Now, I'm an animal lover. Mom raised Persian cats when I was young. Also as a youngster, I had my dog Teddy. I suppose this is where my love of animals stems from. So, it didn't seem in the cards that we would attend one of Mexico City's prime attractions - The Bull Fights. But, it did seem a shame to travel in Mexico and not witness an event unknown in our own country. We opted to go.

We headed for the arena and the place was packed. We had our reserved seats on the shady side. These were more expensive than seats on the sunny side as you might expect because visibility was better and naturally more comfortably cooler in the round, open stadium.

The spectators were completely enthralled by the goings-on judging by their vocalizations. And for us neophytes, the proceedings were exceedingly interesting to watch. There were the processions of picadors, toreadors and matadors dressed in their very colorful and form-fitting costumes. The music was an essential addition to the afternoon's festivities. As to the main event, it was a spectacle about which I'll refrain to comment upon.

It is enough to say that Thelma and I had a full and novel afternoon. I think we both commented, as we made our way back to the hotel, that we were glad to have seen "The Bull Fights" and we will remember them for years to come, but we don't ever wish to attend another. Once was enough.

WATCHED HIGH CLIFF DIVERS, ACAPULCO, MEX. - 1961

On the trip that took Thelma and me to Mexico City, we continued on to Acapulco on the Mexican Pacific coast. I was so happy to go to the famed Mexican Riviera which promised to combine lovely weather, magnificent beaches and on a new ocean for us. We were not disappointed.

Instead of flying there, we decided to take the bus from Mexico City. It proved to be an excellent choice. It was a first class, modern vehicle (no chickens or goats in the passenger compartment!) I don't recall if it was air-conditioned, but I'm sure it must have been. True, the route we traveled took us into the high mountains surrounding MC which are naturally cooler, but we inevitably rode down to sea level on the Pacific coastline.

On the way there, we stopped at one spot for a leg stretch and I couldn't resist taking photos in the beautiful, virtually cloudless and pristine mountain air. It was a gorgeous spot and I'll never forget it.

Eventually we arrived at Acapulco and the place was bustling. We stayed at a fine hotel, the Caleta, alongside the so-called morning beach (because of its orientation towards the morning sun). Of course, we swam there, both at the beach and in the very pretty hotel pool. On other days we taxied to the "afternoon" beach, to the Pacific beaches (Acapulco is mainly on a bay of the big ocean) and, as far as I'm concerned, to the highlight of the trip - a luncheon at La Quebrada where we witnessed the amazing high cliff divers.

The rocky cliffs were a hundred and fifty feet above a small arm of the Pacific. The water they dove into looked as small as a mountain stream, but of course it was deceptively deep. I was to learn later that they timed their dive to coincide with an incoming ocean swell for an added margin of safety. The restaurant had the dining tables situated so that all could see the brave divers do their heart-stopping feat. Other folks watched from a small park opposite the cliffs. It was truly one of my life's most memorable non-ordinary events.

But, alas, it soon came time to leave the magnificent area. On our trip back to MC, we flew. The mountain top views from the plane were scary but interesting. Our flight from Mexico City to Houston was interrupted in mid-flight as poor weather had descended upon Houston. Coming into DC a day late caused me to miss a Washington Redskins football game I had tickets for, but that was the only disappointment for the entire trip.

Acapulco High Cliff Divers

CLIMBED PART OF MAYAN PYRAMID AT CHICHEN ITZA, YUCATAN, MEXICO - 1962 SKINNY-DIPPED OFF COZUMEL ISLAND, YUCATAN, MEX.

Thelma and I loved last year's trip to Mexico so much we decided to do it again. But this time we went to east Mexico, or, namely, the Yucatan Peninsula.

It's hardly a decent flight to fly from Miami, our port of departure in the States, to Mérida in northeast Yucatan, only just over 600 miles. We enjoyed the hotel stay and the horse drawn carriage ride in Mérida as we partook of a guided tour of the city.

In a day or two we were driven to Chichen Itza, site of restored Mayan buildings, pyramids and ball courts. The Mayan civilization was in its heyday at the turn of the century - before the 10th century! The pyramid at Chichen Itza is a marvel of engineering and a sight to behold. It has been named as one of the seven wonders of the western hemisphere and, for what it's worth, I agree. What looked like small steps up its side from a distance were actually rather large steps, but I was determined to scale them at least part way, which I did. I had a sense of accomplishment performing the small feat.

It is my remembrance that the next day we flew to Cozumel Island off the northeast coast of Yucatan. We stayed at a lovely small hotel on the west side of the island with sweet-smelling flowers all around and concrete barstools immersed in the pool. Later we rented bicycles for a trip along the shoreline road. The water was azure blue -- lighter in shade near the shore and a darker color as the calm waters became deeper. I couldn't resist. I had my trunks on so I slipped into the water at a small, isolated beach. Thelma was watching from the shore. About fifty feet out I pulled off my trunks and circled them over my head to Thelma. Thankfully, there were no barracudas around (that I was aware of). It was fun cavorting around without a stitch on for a few minutes or so.

We eventually returned to Mérida from where we toured another Mayan ruin - Uxmal. These buildings, of ceremonial and religious significance were built to survive the ages. Chalk up another satisfying journey for the two of us.

Cozumel, Mexico, Northwest Shore

USHERED OPENING BASEBALL GAME,
DC STADIUM (later RFK) - 1963

I was working in the Pentagon just across the Potomac River from DC in 1963 for the Department of the Army. At the time, the work involved writing army regulations in the area of personnel rules and regulations, answering correspondence, providing data on the subject to colleagues and keeping tabs on material sent to the printer and later distributed, etc.

After the 1961 season, the Washington Senators major league professional baseball team, a team that had been in the "bigs" for a great number of years, was sold off by the owner. The news was quite devastating to most of DC citizens and fans. But, finally, it dawned on most of the Washington VIPs that major league baseball without a team representing the Nation's Capital was unacceptable and therefore temporary. And so, a new team was finally established in DC.

A new stadium was built replacing an old one in midtown where the old Senators held sway (Griffith Stadium). Parking would not now be a problem.

One day, I was approached by a fellow employee. He asked me if I would like to assist as an usher in the Senators opening game in the new stadium on my day off. I jumped at the chance. I don't remember how much it paid or even if it <u>did</u> pay. However, there was no rule that barred us from taking tips if offered.

I had a section of the grandstand which was my "territory". I read people's tickets and escorted them to their assigned seats. I would use my cloth mitt to pull down the seats and dust them off for the patrons. After the game started, there was not much to do besides assisting latecomers to their seats. As a result I saw a good part of that opening game. It was an experience, albeit menial, I'll never forget.

By the way, the brand new stadium was so pretty that day with its emerald green carpet of turf as the focus. The stadium continues to hold ball games, concerts and rallies to this day, although a new team as of 2008, the Nationals, performs in a newer stadium in Southeast Washington.

WATCHED SPORADIC BUT SPECTACULAR GRAND GEYSER ERUPT, YELLOWSTONE, WY. - 1963

This year for my summer vacation I decided to go West. I had heard so much about Yellowstone Park (indeed it is the first national park in the world!); it seemed a great place to recreate. Dad agreed to go also.

We left by car from New York and drove on to Chicago. I had contracted for a trip for two via a railroad (was it the Union Pacific?), to park the car for a week and take the train to Denver. From there we would transfer to a bus for the journey through Colorado and Idaho, passing to the west of the Grand Tetons to Jackson Hole, Wyoming. We stayed overnight in Old Faithful Inn, a fine, rustic accommodation.

This whole area around the Inn seemed like a giant, flat tree-rimmed basin just spouting steam and hot water all over the place. It looked not unlike a railroad yard on a clear, cold day in the days before electrification, except without the dirt and soot.

Promptly at 8 in the morning, a Park Ranger left his spot from behind the Information Counter and announced that the 3-hour, 3-mile walk through the steamy fields would begin. We started out with only about 10 people, but, like the group of children following the piper at Hamelin, we grew.

We walked on 5 foot wide boardwalks which have been put down on the ground all over the area. It is expected that the boardwalks will keep people at a safe distance from the hot springs and geysers and also from the thin mineral crusts which these waters leave when they evaporate.

The Ranger stopped walking every now and then, waited for his straggling group to catch up to him, gave a short talk, answered the numerous questions put to him and then moved on down the boardwalk.

On one occasion, he stopped, we grouped and he talked. Looking at his watch, he said that in a few minutes the small bubbling pool in front of us would erupt. In a few minutes, it erupted. It seemed as if they had turned on a valve back at the Ranger Station. The geyser was a small one - only shot about 10 or 12 feet high - but it <u>was</u> faithful!

On our winding trip, we made a rough circumnavigation of Old Faithful herself. As it goes off about once an hour, we got three different views of the great geyser in action. Each eruption was a little different with each change in light, wind, distance, direction and eruptive power. It's a beautiful thing - so white and graceful against the blue of the sky and the green of the forest.

After awhile, we stopped in front of an area which was at the foot of a small hill. There was a large, gray-green pool in front of us, maybe 20 feet in diameter. Some distance to the left of it were a couple of two foot cones formed through the years by the action of spouting hot water. To the right of the big pool and perhaps 40 feet from it was another small funnel-shaped pool. The green water in it seemed to be rising slowly.

Sitting on the boardwalk were several people, two of whom caught my eye. There was a weather-worn old-timer in working clothes with his suntanned woman by his side. The Ranger later told us that they were geyser hounds - people who sit for hours in front of the less faithful and more spectacular spouters in the expectation of seeing a sight not usually seen by the impatient or less discerning geyser watchers. Some of the more hearty ones of this breed sit for days at this and other geyser holes.

We learned from the Ranger that the big pool was actually the Grand Geyser, a very irregular character. It had been spouting roughly once a day at odd times. When it does erupt, the two cones on the left also erupt; one shoots steam and water constantly during the Grand's eruption to a height of about 12 feet, the other sets in motion in its basin a swirling mass of water and steam three feet high. The Whirlpool Geyser, as the little one is called, also operates about every 20 minutes for a minute during the Grand's dormant stage. Finally, the pool to the right spouts off water and steam irregularly. When it does, however, it's very bad news for Grand Geyser hounds. It apparently relieves the pressure building up in the Grand - action for the right-hand pool means inaction for the big one.

The Ranger asked the old-timer "How's she doing"? He told us that she hadn't spouted in 44 hours and was way overdue, which the Ranger knew. He also said that the right-hand pool was acting up which, of course, was detrimental for the Grand. He was really cussing out the little one.

After further explanations and questions (the smartest ones of which were usually asked by kids), the Ranger said we could keep going on our tour. If Grand did blow, we could come back to it. She never did, that is, that morning. He wound up the walk at about 11.

After lunch, at Old Faithful Inn, I moseyed over to the old master geyser again for its hourly blow. I indicated before how each eruption seemed to be different and why. After Old Faithful's eruption, and it was another beautiful one, I inquired at the Ranger Station as to whether the Grand had gone off. He said no - they're still expecting. I had a little over two hours prior to my bus departure, so I went down to the Grand again.

The old-timers, Pops and his lady, were still there. He asked me if I were going to baby-sit a spell. I said I thought I'd give it a half hour or so and sat down. A few other people were gathering around - some on the walk, others on the hill to the rear of the pool, almost all with cameras.

Pops told me that the funnel pool to the right seemed to be calming down more, although when I passed her, she was full to the brim. The whirler to the left was popping off every 20 minutes on schedule, spilling its water into the pool of the Grand. The pool of the Grand, consequently, was quietly overflowing a bit. Pops thought he detected a greater overflow than usual once, but nothing came of it.

Another Ranger came up to inspect the Grand's possibilities. This in itself was a good omen to Pops. The Ranger, carrying a notebook, would gingerly walk up closer to the pool of the Grand and peer in, walk a little closer still staring intently at the water with the whiffs of steam wafting off the surface. But he turned around, shrugged his shoulders and came back to the walk. After a few minutes, he gave up and left.

It was peaceful there. The sky was solid blue, the sun was burning hot but the breeze on our backs was cool. There was very little sound - a bird now and then, the clomp, clomp, clomp of a family walking by on the boardwalk, the 20 minute eruptions at the Whirlpool Geyser. But mostly, it was quiet and peaceful - and time consuming.

I had learned earlier that the Riverside Geyser, one of the most dependable in the Park, was due to blow at 2:30. The Riverside is a unique geyser in that it spews at an angle out over the Firehole River. This I'd wanted to see. Also, I guess that the damn Grand Geyser had beaten me. But after I had started out for the Riverside, I figured that by the time I had watched it and then had begun the long walk back to the Inn, I might be in danger of missing my bus. I decided to go back to the Grand for a few more minutes of observation.

The small pool to the right was quiet but everything else was normal. It did seem like the pool of the Grand was oozing more water over its sides than it had earlier. The runoff stream seemed fuller. Pops noticed this too. He seemed to be more animated now. It's been 48 hours since the last eruption, the runoff is heavier, the reliever is practically dormant. He was positive it would go within minutes.

The first thing I noticed was that the runoff was positively building up. Then in quick succession, bubbles appeared in the middle of the pool of the Grand, the Whirlpool gushed up and out heavily, and then she started. A few feet at first, but she started.

The old-timer was really excited, jumping up and down, yelling that he'd been here since 5 this morning and finally got to see the Grand play. He ran back of the walk, away from the Grand, to get better camera shots. I did too.

She started up slowly, practically the whole pool of water I mean. But then she narrowed and went high into the air, each drop sparkling silver in the bright sun against the sky, big white clouds of steam burping out of the water. People were all on their feet now, the hounds as well as the lucky stiffs who just happened to clomp by at the right time. The 12 foot geyser on the left, called the Vent, was also spewing a forceful combination of steam and water.

The Grand continued for about a minute, about as high as Old Faithful herself and then she slackened off slowly to a few bubbles. The Vent and the Whirlpool kept going. People had been genuinely awed.

Then up rose the Grand again after a minute's rest. This time it seemed higher. It looked for all the world like a giant fireworks display. Upon intensive examination, the geyser spout was made up of hundreds of shoots of water, each shoot made up of individual drops of water each reaching higher into the deep blue sky. It continued like this, with the Vent and the Whirlpool still going, for another minute and then she subsided again.

After another relatively quiet minute, she roared into the air a third time, this time higher than the second time and even more spectacularly. It differed from Old Faithful's spout mostly by diverging more. Whereas Old Faithful's spout is straight and true until slowly bent over backwards by wind and gravity, the Grand's spout was like a giant lady's fan which is held upright but only partly open at the top.

A crowd was beginning to gather as the news of the Grand's eruption was spreading throughout the valley. The people just kept repeating over and over 'It's amazing, it's beautiful'.

The Grand erupted ten separate times with each eruption going higher than the last. I noticed that when she rested for a minute between eruptions the level of the water in the pool was reduced. The Vent and the Whirlpool continued in full force during the whole show. After some twenty-odd minutes, Vent and Whirlpool finally weakened and the Grand rose no more. The time was so short before my bus was to leave that I couldn't remain a second longer. But I had seen a magnificent and exciting sight of nature and one which is not usually seen without an effort.

Back on the bus, I found myself reluctant to tell others of my unforgettable experience, except my dad, partly because I feared that others would not share my excitement and joy, and partly because I feared they would not believe me.

WORKED IN PENTAGON FOR DEPARTMENT OF THE ARMY - 1963

As mentioned previously, I came to Washington, DC to obtain employment with the Census Bureau, a part of the Department of Commerce. When the 1950 Census was all but over, I looked around for a federal job in the field of personnel, the better to utilize my university major and minor in psychology and statistics. I wound up with the Department of the Army in the Defense Department.

In 1952 after I left Census, I became a part of the Adjutant General's Office of the Department of the Army. It so happened that my first job had me working with others interviewing army personnel to determine the specifics of their duties and writing up army job specifications based on those and other interviews. Later I became more involved in the area of personnel testing.

This work was in an office not located in the Pentagon, but in a "tempo" building, as we called it, in northeast Washington. The tempos were erected as a result of the WW II build up which required a large increase in personnel and office space. We worked in several tempos before finally winding up in the famed Pentagon itself in 1963.

I was generally amazed at the size of that place. I would habitually take a walk after lunch and systematically observe every floor and ring of the building over a period of months. Also, as far as I could, I inspected the large basement area, the outer grounds on all five sides and, finally, the inner court. The building never ceased to impress me. The parking lots were enormous (hope you brought your umbrella if it was raining). The main corridors were wide enough to drive trucks through. I worked in the Pentagon for eleven years to top off a 22 year career with the Army Department.

I would have to say, looking back at the experience, that, despite the enormity of the building, working there was, on the whole, a rewarding occupation. One never had a feeling of being lost in the vast labyrinth or being swallowed up by a massive edifice. The building, only four stories high, required no public elevators and left minimal degradation of the Potomac River skyline.

Pentagon Award Presentation

SAW SOLAR ECLIPSE FROM RAILWAY DOME CAR, NEBRASKA - 1963

On the way back from our Yellowstone National Park trip, we rode from Denver to Chicago (where our car was parked and waiting) in train seats that converted to upper and lower berths. Dad took the lower, I, the upper. Don't know about dad, but I slept quite nicely.

Several cars away were the dining car and the food was fine. But the train feature that primarily attracted my attention was the observation car at the tail end of the train. The seats were comfortable and higher than normal railway seats. The observation car had a dome on it allowing unobstructed 180 degree visibility - just excellent.

We rode across the Nebraska plains during the day and got our fill of wheat fields. But every so often we would pass through a town to break up the grain plain. Two particular events occurred, one in the evening and one in broad daylight. The evening event was a series of thunder (and lightning) storms roaming over the super flat plains some miles from our moving vantage point. It was a poor man's version of a fireworks show, but just about as spectacular.

The daytime show was, of course, the partial eclipse of the sun on Thursday, July 11, 1963. I don't recall any of the particulars of the eclipse, i.e., the percentage of solar obscuration at maximum or temperature fluctuation outside the railroad car. But the view through our over-exposed photo film was beautiful and the setting only added to the gorgeous event. Eventually, we reached Chicago, retrieved our VW and headed home to New York and home for dad. I left for Washington, DC a day later.

Both of us could hardly wait to tell his daughter, my sister, about our wonderful adventure through the heartland of the great USA, topped off with an eclipse of our life-supporting solar orb.

FLEW DC TO NY TO SEE BROADWAY PLAY 'HOW TO SUCCEED . . .' ON DAY AFTER ASSASSINATION OF PRESIDENT KENNEDY - 1963

Friday, November 22, 1963 was indeed a black day in US history as President John F. Kennedy was shot as he rode in a motorcade through Dallas, Texas. He died later in the hospital. Weeks before I had bought two tickets to see the Broadway show 'How To Succeed In Business Without Really Trying'. The date my girlfriend Thelma and I were to fly to New York from Washington, DC to see the musical was November 23.

I called the New York theater to ascertain if the show would go on Saturday, the day after the assassination and they said it would. The following Monday, however, the theater would be dark in remembrance of the fallen leader.

Like just about everyone else, 45 years later I can recall exactly what I was doing when the horrible deed was perpetrated. I was working in the Pentagon and I had just come back from lunch. I took a short walk outside the building on the side where the Pentagon heliport was located. I passed by a window of the building and someone had put up a makeshift brown paper sign and had it taped to the glass. It was written with a black marker pen and indicated "KENNEDY SHOT". Since it hit me completely out of the blue, I could not believe it at first. I hustled back to my desk where I found out that it was unfortunately true. Some television sets were on by now and we learned the awful truth that the president was dead.

In NY the next day, Thelma and I walked from the airport bus stop to the theater west of Broadway. We saw many an office and storefront window sign expressing sympathy, condolences and remembrances to the Kennedy family and to the country as a whole.

At the theater (it was a Saturday matinee performance); a minute of silence was held to honor the stricken President of the United States. The show was a good one with lots of songs and jokes which seemed incongruous then, but, as the saying goes, life (and the show) must go on. It is still hard to believe that the monstrous deed occurred at all.

DROVE THROUGH SNOWSTORM, DC TO NY, TO BOARD HMS QUEEN ELIZABETH FOR TRIP TO BAHAMAS - 1964

WITNESSED FROM SHIPBOARD, DEPARTURE OF LINER QUEEN ELIZABETH FROM HUDSON RIVER NYC DOCK WITHOUT AID OF TUGBOATS

The trip started at 4 in the morning on a wet, cold February day. Packed bags, all labeled in accordance with Cunard Steamship Line's instructions, were loaded into the VW and off we went - my girlfriend and I.

In Washington, DC the snow was falling hard but the streets were merely wet, shiny and glistening in the purple glow of the new-fangled sodium vapor street lamps. Speeding along the dark and lonely parkway to Baltimore, the snow became less wet and more white. The Bug's headlights bored their way through scurrying and relentless streaks of white.

In a short while Baltimore was left behind thanks to the tunnel beneath its harbor. As the distance to New York City lessened, the snow on the ground became thicker. Speed had to be reduced as traction became more of a problem. But the Queen Elizabeth was lying at Pier 92, North River with a sailing time of 11:30 AM and a "get on board" time of 8:30. Speed had to be maintained. Except for a quartering wind, the toughest part of the operation was passing the monster trucks and trailers, with their 18 wheels spinning up blinding clouds of fallen precipitation.

The black sky turned gray near the Delaware Memorial Bridge, a dark gray but a gray. The New Jersey Turnpike had a 35 MPH speed limit posted from the very beginning. But to do the 110 mile trip at 35 would be cutting it to fine. To top it off, some kindly radio announcer said there was a mile-long traffic tie-up at the Lincoln Tunnel entrance, our gateway to the big city. So it was push ahead, pass everything (including jack-knifed and up-ended rigs) and hope for the best. A quick hot breakfast on the way helped relieve the strain.

Trenton, Elizabeth, Newark, Jersey City turnoffs were passed; Lincoln Tunnel traffic proved normal and the tunnel was happily entered offering a brief respite from those swirling flakes and buffeting winds; the Big Apple's vehicle and snow-choked streets were traversed. But finally, there she was - black, white and beautiful - the stately Queen E. It was almost 11 AM.

Down in the lobby forward of the main lounge a blackboard indicated that sailing time had been pushed back to 2:30 PM to accommodate weather-caused late arrivers. Now they tell me!

I was mostly interested in getting topside and observing the Queen moving out of the harbor without the aid of tugs. The "tuggers" were on strike. I found a protected spot forward, under the bridge. The whole process seemed deceptively simple. The lines were released by the pier hands and hauled aboard on large electrically driven winches. The ship then inched its way backward and out into the river at an agonizingly slow pace. Many of the deck hands were shoveling and washing the snow and slush off the bow area where a lot of the business of running the ship takes place. Slowly we turned downstream, passed the midtown Manhattan skyline fathered by the Empire State Building, passed the Wall Street skyline which appears to rise straight out of the water, passed the watchful Liberty statue and passed the busy Staten Island ferries. Looming ahead was the under-construction Verrazano Bridge crossing the narrows. It is so imposing it pales all other features of the vista at this point. All of our eyes (other people were as interested in the process as I was) were on the top of the forward mast as we approached the bridge at a smart pace now. It certainly appeared as if we were too tall to fit under. I suppose it's very deceptive from our vantage point, but it certainly did not seem like there was more than 3 or 4 feet between the bottom of the Verrazano and the top of Elizabeth's mast. Now, there was nothing but open sea ahead of us.

In two days the Queen lay motionless in the warm sunshine outside Nassau harbor in the Bahamas. We could take advantage of the tender service which transported passengers from ship to shore on a regular schedule. We caught the 9:00 o'clock and it gave us our first chance to see our Queen from a distance and a great sight she was; black down from A Deck with the hundreds of portholes all aligned so neatly and the rest of the ship all white and clean with the two massive black and orange stacks at a rakish angle. The icing on the cake was a line of crazily-colored pennants from the bow to the top of the forward mast to the aft mast to the stern all waving languidly in the semi-tropical breeze.

In Nassau, we got into Cadillacs for our guided tour. We saw stuffy old forts and spiffy new hotels, ramshackle houses and the resplendent Governor's Mansion with the statue of Christopher Columbus in white marble in front. And through the coconut palms we could always catch a glimpse of our floating hotel laying at anchor in the harbor.

After the auto tour, some of us took a boat to Paradise Island for some swimming. The beach is well named, a beautiful crescent of white sand slipping gradually into darkening blue water. The rear of the strand was rimmed with the ever-present palm trees. The facilities at this beach were spacious and immaculate. And the sun was hot and bright as we lolled about on the fiber mats. In the distance, still watching over her subjects, was her serene highness, the Queen Elizabeth. After a swim in the fine, clear water and a spell of beachcombing, we headed back to Nassau, to the wharf, to the ship and to the dinner plate.

The meal devoured, the cigarette finished, the coffee cup drained, off we'd go for the evening's activities, being careful to say 'Good Evening' back to the little boy at the door and to grab a few dinner mints from the silver tray in the vestibule.

The evening's activity was the first run movie "Seven Days In May" - a very good one - and going from bar to bar sampling the entertainment and an occasional drink. It turned out to be the best damn old George Washington's birthday celebration I ever had (hic). It was good to get back to the bunk that night.

Waiting around the pier for the return tender the next day, I watched a new Ford being off-loaded in a rope cradle from a ship, a Bahamian cop dressed in a khaki uniform with his belly oozing out over his belt, a couple of brown, slender youths diving for coins from their rowboat, a group of dilapidated but colorful fishing boats where all hands were preparing their catch for market and a sleek white and brown yacht slipping through the ripples on its way to open sea.

After the evening's dinner, the choice was between seeing "From Russia With Love" a rip-snorting James Bond adventure in the theater or shipping into Nassau to see some limbo dancers at places like the Junkanoo, the Cat and the Fiddle, or even Dirty Dicks. Unfortunately, the lure of the movie proved too strong; Bahamian night life will have to be sampled on another trip. But the flick <u>was</u> good and we later notched off a couple more of the ship's 14 bars.

Sunday morning was hazy bright as we plowed northward through the Atlantic for home port.

Awake at 6 the last morning, I dressed warmly and went up on deck to "stand my watch". It was jet black outside except for some distant shore lights. The Queen was moving more slowly, waiting, I guess, to time its movement into the NY Narrows and up the North (Hudson) River and home. Tide, daylight and landing details are all considerations in this operation.

The stars began to ease away in the gray light of dawn when, lo and behold, there she was - the mighty Verrazano Narrows Bridge - bedecked with a bead of lights from Brooklyn to Staten Island. The bridge is truly an impressive sight even in the dark. The only sad thing about it, I think, is that it will certainly come to dwarf the Statue of Liberty, up the harbor several miles, into relative insignificance as the New York port of entry's premier landmark.

We glided slowly and silently under the raw steel girders in the cold gray dawn. The only sound I heard up on the Sports Deck next to the giant funnels was a distant "clangal-dang-clangal" of a buoy channel marker and the quiet spooky moan of the wind through the rigging. In the Upper Bay of the New York harbor, the ever-busy ferries were slapping their way through the choppy water going to and from the isles of Manhattan and Staten.

At this point, to starboard was a dark Brooklyn beneath a brightening and partly cloudy sky; ahead was the impressive and unbelievable sight of the tall slabs of stone and glass of lower Manhattan rising out of the water; and to port, the graceful and patient lady with the torch and book. And still we slid north slowly and silently.

We moved up the river to midtown Manhattan and 49th Street and our forward motion ceased. There were no tugboats about so apparently it would be a tugless docking operation. I was shivering by this time but I couldn't leave now. The docking proceeded flawlessly it seemed to me, but I was cold. I went to breakfast and lots of hot coffee.

After breakfast there were many details concerning debarking, luggage, customs (another cold hour in the drafty building on the pier), retrieving the car, getting it loaded and driving it out of the place. Considering that a heck of a lot of people had to have a heck of a lot of luggage moved off the ship, claimed by owners, inspected and stashed away in a heck of a lot of vehicles in a rather cramped area, it all went off remarkably well.

On the way back to Washington (no snow this time), I paid the price for my morning's vigil in the cold air by sniffling and sneezing through most of the trip.

But it was a fine five days. I don't believe five days were ever spent filled with so much interesting activity. We had enough to think about, talk about, reminisce about for years to come, my girlfriend and I.

Ready for Formal Dinner, HMS QUEEN ELIZABETH

Thelma Martin at Bahamian Straw Market

LIVED IN APARTMENT TEN BLOCKS FROM U.S. CAPITOL BUILDING - 1965

Two years after the Kennedy assassination, Thelma and I decided to move to the "new" Southwest section of Washington, DC. Prior to the move, we lived in separate locations, she in the Northwest quadrant of the city and I in the Northeast. Every evening I would drive over to her place and stay until breakfast once we got to realize that we were compatible.

In the 1950's, DC decided to raze the largely dilapidated area in the Southwest quadrant and replace it with modern high-rise and two story apartments and condominiums. This appealed to us as we thought we could rent separate apartments in the same high-rise building - I opted for an efficiency apartment on the fourth floor, she a one bedroom place on the first floor. With this arrangement we had our own separate addresses and mail boxes, but only had to use the elevator to see one another.

The apartments - Carrollsburg Square by name - later converted to condominiums which we continued to occupy. It was a great arrangement for the both of us as we both had our separate careers - working for Uncle Sam's federal government. Although I met Thelma when we were both working at the Census Bureau, we soon went our separate ways in our employment situation, she to the Department of Health and Human Services and I to the Department of the Army.

The south wing of the Capitol Building is on Independence Avenue (originally B Street). And we were on M Street, a difference of eleven blocks. Since there is no J Street (for some reason), the difference in blocks is only ten.

I had many a walk around the Capitol and its environs "on the hill" as they say (we lived in the Southwest for almost 30 years, she for 28 and I for 32). It always made me swell with pride to be so close to the heart of the nation, to the House of Representatives, to the Senate, the Supreme Court and the Library of Congress.

RODE MOTORBIKE ON THE BEACH
AT DAYTONA BEACH, FLORIDA - 1967

While working in the Pentagon, I spotted an upcoming vacation trip to Florida. The excursion would entail traveling by train on the Atlantic Coast Line to northeastern Florida and from there we would take side trips to St. Augustine, to the John F. Kennedy Space Center at Cape Canaveral and to Daytona Beach.

St. Augustine, the oldest city in the US, was delightful as we saw the town and fort using horse and buggy transportation. The weather was perfect and the town was beautiful. In the trip to the Space Center, we utilized people-mover vehicles to see the monstrously large hangars which housed the massive space rockets. The difference between space shots on television and eying the rockets first hand is, well, eye-opening.

But, I think, my most enjoyable time was spent at Daytona Beach. We stayed there for one or two days at a motel on the beach. The motel pool was a beautiful one and gave us a chance to grab a few Florida rays and swim a lap or two. I can remember lounging on the pool furniture and getting excited when a group of four pelicans cruised overhead searching for God knows what - food, I suppose. Then maybe twenty minutes later you would see the big birds soaring back to where they had originated. We don't see that kind of stuff in Washington!

But one morning, we, and when I say we I mean the other members of the tour group, walked to the beach proper and decided to rent motorbikes. As is well known, Daytona Beach has cement-like sand, hard enough to drive cars and motorbikes on. One of the girls in the group didn't want to drive the bike, but wanted to ride on one. So I offered, generous as I am, to let her ride behind me on the scooter. She held on to me close and tight and we rode up the beach and back, stopping at our motel for a drink. It was a satisfying interlude which led to nothing. All too soon we had to leave the Sunshine State and entrain back to our busy, urban and "pelicanless" world, but refreshed.

SKIED FOR WEEK IN CANADIAN LAURENTIANS, QUEBEC - 1968

Thelma and I had zero experience with skiing, but we were young (relatively). I spied this vacation trip to a place I had heard much about - the Canadian Laurentians (mountains) in Quebec. The trip promised a week of "Ski School" and seemed like a lot of fun.

We went north by train out of DC and New York. Riding the rails along the east side of the Hudson provided a beautiful panorama of views. As a boy I had taken numerous trips up and down the river by Hudson River Day Line boats, one of which was mentioned earlier. Many memories flooded back. I don't recall passing Lake Champlain on this trip, but the lake's length is 600 miles and on a direct path to Montreal, our interim destination.

At the Montreal train station, we eventually joined our group going to Mont Tremblant in the Laurentians. At the Ski School (L'Ecole de Ski du Mont Tremblant) we were greeted warmly and a good thing. The temperature was freezing - just right for skiing. The main lodge of the skiing complex was all one could hope for - log-hewn rustic, giant central fireplace, inviting drinking areas and comfortable if sturdy furniture.

The toughest part of the first morning was applying the layers of clothing paraphernalia we had and which were needed. On the slopes, we received our first lesson - side-slipping, snow plowing, negotiating uphill climbs on skis, controlling downhill motion with ski poles, and most important, how to get yourself upright after falling! Our instructor was excellent. I caught on fairly quickly, but Thelma, bless her heart, didn't immediately move on to the next (intermediate) class.

I continued on and really enjoyed the freedom and joy of sliding down the mountain under control with the frosty air in my face. We were to enjoy many ski trail runs for the next few days. The final morning's class was a thrilling ride down Mont Tremblant's longest and steepest run, combining scenery, tree areas, turns and heart-stopping direct descents - really exciting activity.

On the final morning before departure, there was at least one guy I saw who had so much fun on the trip, he signed up on the spot for another one in the near future. We also had a graduation from Ski School ceremonial luncheon. We all received our diplomas, yes, even Thelma, who probably put in more time at the lodge than on the slopes. All in all it was a sensational trip for me and I think for my companion too.

Ski Week, Mont Tremblant, Canada

SAW PERFECT TOTAL SOLAR ECLIPSE, SANDBRIDGE, VA - 1970

In Washington, DC I asked my girlfriend Thelma Martin, if she would like to see a total solar eclipse. She asked me "When do we start?"

We would be heading south to near Norfolk, Virginia, some 190 miles distant. Our plan would be to fly to Norfolk, rent a car and drive to near Sandbridge Beach some 20 miles to the southeast on the Atlantic coast.

Saturday, March 7, 1970 dawned bright, clear and warm for early March in Washington, DC. We left from National Airport in nearby Virginia and followed our plan to the letter, arriving near Sandbridge Beach about lunchtime. I saw a spot in a clearing which provided an unobstructed view of most of the horizon and higher. Thelma had packed a lunch for us which we ate in the car with no interference from the curious.

The spot was idyllic - somewhat off the road, no one around and clear in all directions. To tell the truth, I expected visitors, fellow eclipse chasers or the idly curious, but very few came around during the three or four hours we were there.

The weather conditions were practically perfect. The sky was blue, the temperature was 54 degrees at eclipse time with virtually no wind, eclipse time was early to mid-afternoon (1:30 PM) and we were sitting smack dab on the center line of a total solar eclipse. Finally, the eclipse would be at a perfect angle in the sky - above the horizon haze, but below the neck straining zenith. It promised to be the perfect eclipse.

I had brought my household thermometer in order to plot temperatures before, during and after the big event. Of course, partiality came first and after a period of time, totality hit us smack in our faces. The black disk with the pearly corona lasted nearly three minutes. This is the time when no eye protection is needed. The lowest temperature I recorded was 38 degrees. This was our first ever total eclipse. Would we ever see another as spectacular? Hell, would we ever see another?

After an hour or so, the temperature had returned to its pre-eclipse reading - 55 degrees to be exact. Nothing to do now but pack up and head back to Norfolk. We went over to the ocean at the beach and then headed north through Virginia Beach before arriving at the Norfolk airport. We were home in several hours which only added to the perfection of the event. I suppose there was another element which added to the perfect day. We had done the whole affair on our own

- planning to be at the right place and time and carrying out our modest plan flawlessly. I really had a sense of accomplishment that evening. It was quite an eclipse and trip.

BICYCLED FROM DC TO
MOUNT VERNON, VA AND BACK - 1970

I had heard about this bicycle and walking path which was laid out by the local and federal governments. It took advantage of existing streets, sidewalks and paths. It traversed Memorial Bridge, followed Alexandria's streets, went through parks, along highways, passed the periphery of Ronald Reagan National Airport (then Washington National Airport), alongside Virginia marinas, through wooded areas until it approached George Washington's home at Mount Vernon. The total one-way distance was about 25 miles.

I rented a bicycle in DC and headed for Memorial Bridge - the ceremonial bridge leading to the National Cemetery, John F. Kennedy's grave and eternal flame and Robert E. Lee's Arlington House on top of the hill overlooking Washington. Soon the bicycle path was skirting the airport and heading to the colonial town of Alexandria where the prominent architectural theme is red and buff-colored brick.

Passed Alexandria, the path provided more distant views of the Potomac River, temperate-zone wooded areas and suburbs. Eventually I reached our first president's home, in a beautiful, high, grass covered location overlooking a giant bend in the Potomac.

Facilities were provided to stash your bike securely, permitting roaming around the houses and grounds unencumbered. There was a lot to see; gardens, farmed areas (saw a sheep shearing), kitchens near but not in the main house, slave quarters, storage houses for food provisions and graveyards. The main house itself had a long back porch filled with chairs where one could relax and gaze at the Potomac and the boats upon it, drifting up and down the river. The opposite shore (Maryland) was covered with the natural green growth of trees, bushes and grass.

But soon it was time to depart, retrieve my transportation and head north for the District of Columbia and home. Once again I seemed to acquire that sense of adventure, admittedly less than major, which provided me with a self-satisfying glow. Got to do this again sometime.

SPENT NEW YEAR'S EVE IN THE HEAT OF CARTAGENA, COL. - 1970

We had heard about this trip down South America way to Cartagena, Colombia on the Caribbean coast. It sounded intriguing especially since it was to occur over the New Year's holiday. Some friends of Thelma's and mine would also go.

Cartagena was an important seaport during the Spanish colonial days. They shipped much of the treasure they acquired from the New World back to Spain from the fine, easily protected harbor of the city. We took the city tour which included a stop at a fort on a high peak in the city overlooking the harbor. On another day, we visited the surrounding countryside where we saw farms and craftsmen plying their wares. A swim in the bay later helped to cool things off for us.

On a third day, we traveled by boat across the wide harbor waters to a park near the open Caribbean. They told us how, in the old days, a heavy chain was placed across a narrow entrance to the harbor to further protect the city from marauding pirates. At one point Thelma had a call of nature and inquired about the boat's facilities. The deck hand pointed to the rear where a board was situated just behind the rear transom. She decided to wait.

But the highlight of the trip was the New Year's Eve supper and celebration. We had a fine time between the eating, the entertainment and the ringing in of the new 1971, but it was hot. There was no air-conditioning and, well, it was hot. I suppose this was the warmest New Year's Eve I've ever had and, furthermore, ever likely to have in the future. But, what counts, I suppose, is we all had a good time. The trip was educational and a lot of fun.

FORDED SOUTH BRANCH, POTOMAC RIVER ON HORSEBACK, W.V. - 1971

On the second phase of my horseback riding experiences, I spied a trip arranged by the Sierra Club. It would start in Berkeley Springs in northeast West Virginia and roam through the Cacapon Mountains. We camped out between visiting several sites during the week on our animals. I was fitted with a noble steed named 'Goliath'. He was large, befitting my 6 foot frame, but not as large as his name would suggest.

Some of our visited sites included the Paw Paw tunnel near Paw Paw, an old but working farmhouse in the mountains, a climb up a promontory overlooking a compound bend in the Potomac River (a magnificent view with a scary but necessary trip on horseback, of course, down a steep mountainside where you had to lean back in the saddle quite a bit) and a rubber raft trip on some 'white water' which was on the tame side but offered a welcome respite from the back of poor Goliath. Four days on the animal by an office worker showed me some muscles I never knew I had.

The real fun on the trip for me was the fording of a branch of the Potomac River by horse, just like they do in the western movies! The branch of the river was maybe 200 feet wide and no more than four feet deep, I would say. To keep from getting (too) wet, we had to pull up our feet while they were still in the stirrups, not exactly easy. And so our tenderfoot group negotiated the water barrier without losing a single man or woman! We did have a few more engrossing tales to tell that evening, however.

It was great getting back to civilization four days later to our motel and a nifty lake swim. Since we were without the benefit of showers for the horseback trip and the weather had turned warmer, the water felt especially fine. So phase II of my equine activities was accomplished; next year it will be a trip through Yellowstone Park by horse, saddle and tent. It will have to go some to supply the fun and experience of this West Virginia - Cacapon Mountain - expedition.

ICE-SKATED ON REFLECTING POOL NEAR LINCOLN MEMORIAL, DC - 1972

I suppose at this age I'm in my adventurous days. I just wanted to do anything and everything (within reason) I hadn't done before. One of those things was ice skating.

Oh, as a kid, we used to go up to Van Cortlandt Park in The Bronx and ice skate there with rented skates. Also I can remember when I was working as an insurance clerk in NY prior to my federal government service, I made a date with one of my fellow employees, Dolores Biancomano by name, to ice skate in Central Park in Manhattan. We had a lot of fun.

But that was 23 years earlier. I wanted to do some skating now that I was a mature man.

In Washington, they had located an ice skating rink just south of the National Archives Building at Constitution Avenue and Seventh Street, NW. So, I purchased a pair of skates and tried my hand again at sliding over the ice on steel blades. At first, it was a little daunting. Ice skating when you were younger and then, after a period of years, not doing the activity at all, takes a little reeducation. I can swear I detected some of the younger girls snickering at my efforts, but perhaps it was my imagination.

But there came a time when the weather turned really cold for an extended period of time, and it doesn't happen often in Washington, DC. The reflecting pool between the Washington Monument and the Lincoln Memorial not only freezes over, but forms ice multiple inches thick. This year the time had come. The Park Department determined that the pool ice had to be 4 inches thick or more. It was cold enough for that to occur at this time. So off I went with my ice skates to glide across the ice on the Reflecting Pool.

I must say the ice was not all that smooth. They had no machinery to smooth the ice, like a Zamboni. So one had to watch as he skated. But there I was, with the orange sun setting slowly behind the Lincoln Memorial in the icy air, skating away like a happy Norwegian. When I decided to rest for awhile, the Park people had set up a metal drum with holes in the sides and filled with yellow and glowing embers. Life is good when you're having fun.

TOOK HORSEBACK TRIP THROUGH YELLOWSTONE PARK, WY. - 1972

BATHED IN HOT SPRING IN WOODS, YELLOWSTONE PARK, WY.

It's time for the big one. I've been working up to take this Yellowstone National Park horseback trip for more than a year. It's a week in length and in order that I can fit right in out West, I get me a big old cowboy hat and riding boots to go with my blue jeans, checkered shirts and bandana. I tell you I'm set.

I fly to Denver wearing my ten gallon hat - well, it doesn't fit in my pocket now does it? Thelma sees me off at Dulles International Airport near DC. From Denver I fly to Jackson Hole, Wyoming. Soon we meet up with our guides who will supply the horses, tents and grub and who will be with us for the week. Then, it's a matter of matching horse with rider and listening to the do's and don'ts of trail riding in the park. Two of the rules; at a break, ladies to the left and men to the right of the trail and don't leave anything behind in the park but your footsteps.

The first night in the tents it was so peaceful and quiet and beautiful in the twilight. The next morning at breakfast, one of the youngsters swears he heard a bear checking out his digs. The guide said that it could have been.

On the trail the next day we were headed for Yellowstone Lake. We would be camping near the shore. About halfway there, we had to stand aside. The camp hands had the tough job of breaking the old camp, packing all the gear on mules, catching up with us on the trail and getting to the new camp area in time to set it up prior to our arrival. Quite a job, I would say. But it was so thrilling to see that mule team and their leaders and their load hurrying along the trail to beat us to the camp site at the lake.

I remember going to a stream to wash up a bit in the cold, clear mountain stream. It was invigorating. On another day we made camp near Mt. Sheridan, I guess the highest peak in Yellowstone. We eventually went to the top. There was a ranger station there with a fire tower. Any smoke detected in the woods would be reported to the proper authorities.

Near this camp, maybe a mile or two away, was a stream of boiling water emanating from the ground. As the stream worked its way lower, it would gradually cool, of course. So it was possible to pick a portion of the stream that contained water the exact temperature you might desire. With permission, I took off one afternoon with my steed to take a hot Yellowstone bath. I think my horse was a little reluctant about the whole thing, what with leaving his buddies and all. On the way back, he fairly galloped to join up with his trail pals. But I was clean. Eventually, we returned to civilization all suntanned and ready to take on John Wayne!

Yellowstone Horse Pack Trip

RODE STEAM LOCOMOTIVE TRAIN - ALEXANDRIA, VA TO FRONT ROYAL, VA AND BACK - 1972

We heard about this upcoming day trip that would take us west from nearby Alexandria, Virginia to Front Royal, VA, near the Blue Ridge Parkway, a distance of some 60 miles one-way. This trip would be by train - a train pulled by a steam locomotive.

In these years, steam locomotives are a rarity; they're just about all gone. All the railroads have gone diesel or electric. That's what made this trip so distinctive - a smoke-billowing, steam-pulsing, steam-whistle blowing, black locomotive. In my younger days they were the railroads power engine - there was no alternative. They powered the westward movement of this country. But these days, they're a wonder and a curiosity to the young folk. We thought it would be a hoot to go on this trip.

We caught the train in the Alexandria train depot. It was somewhat scary to see the big engine coming passed us, hissing and panting, into the station. Once we were settled in, we inspected the train. They had regular closed coaches and a car with an open platform. This car permitted photographers, of which there were many, to snap away unobstructed to their heart's content.

Maybe an hour into the trip the train stopped in an open field. Folks could get off the train, the train would back up and then come roaring back past us. The smoke was billowing from the stack and the whistle was doing its thing. That's a sound I miss from my childhood, a good old fashioned steam locomotive whistle. Of course, all the shutterbugs took advantage of this "flying pass" to record the speeding train on film. The train then backed up a second time to pick us up and we all piled onto the train to continue on to Front Royal.

At Front Royal we had lunch, inspected the engine up close, the railway station and the town. Then soon we were headed back to Alexandria and DC.

It was an exciting trip. We went on the trip with one of Thelma's girlfriends and her young son. The boy loved it, but the mom happened to wear a white suit which gathered a lot of soot from the trip. I don't think she'll be wearing white again on another steam locomotive excursion - if there ever is one in the future.

STOOD ONE HOUR WATCH AT HELM OF THREE-MASTED SAILING SHIP ON CARIBBEAN WATERS - 1973

SAW GREEN FLASH AT SUNSET, CARIBBEAN SEA

Out of nowhere, Thelma and I, after reading the literature, decided to go on this so-called "Barefoot Cruise" this year. It really seemed like a great adventure; we would fly to San Juan, Puerto Rico, then, after a few days there, where we would meet the cruise's owner, fly on to Antigua. In Antigua, a former British possession, we would embark on a three-masted schooner and sail the Caribbean. Sound good? Well it was all of that.

Whenever Thelma and I went on a trip together, we almost always had separate rooms. We finally felt bold enough, on this rugged cruise, to occupy the same living quarters - in this case a ships cabin. The rooms were small as were the bunks, but I didn't lose any sleep that week.

You didn't have to, but if you wished to, you could help out as a deckhand. I, for instance, took a watch at the helm one early morning for an hour. I can confirm that I did not run the schooner on to the rocks at any time, although getting the hang of turning the helm one way to steer the ship the other way took a bit of getting used to.

Our itinerary took us from Antigua down the Leeward Islands. We made ports-of-call at Iles de Saintes, St. Lucia, St. Vincent, Bequia, Carriacou, Grenada, Mayreau, Martinique, Dominica and back to Antigua to complete our trip. Each stop was a very interesting interlude.

We met really fascinating people as you might expect. One 'barefooter' was a bachelor girl from Montreal named Margaret Curwen. She was originally from England and an RN. Margaret, sometime later, stayed at Thelma's place in DC and in 1976 we stayed at her place in Montreal when we attended the Olympic Games.

There were so many remarkable episodes in the trip, but I will only mention one - the green flash. As we watched one of the sunsets, one more gorgeous than the other, we waited for the very final moment when the limb of the orange ball would sink beneath the watery horizon. If you watched closely, you might see this fleeting green flash of light and then no more sun for the day. It was very subtle but definite - and awesome. It was another out-of-the-ordinary event which will stay in my memory as long as I live.

'Barefoot' Cruise Captain on the Job

Gorgeous Caribbean Sunset

RETIRED FROM FEDERAL SERVICE AFTER 27 YEARS OF SERVICE - 1974

I don't recall much of the ceremony which was conducted to present me with my Certificate of Retirement on my 51st birthday. There were also many kind words uttered by our organizational leaders in addition to Certificates of Appreciation.

I do remember unexpectedly receiving a beautiful piece of luggage from Thelma Martin who was working in the Department of Health and Human Services at the time. She had it delivered to the office in a timely fashion. By way of reciprocation, when she retired from federal service some years later, I made it my business to have a big, gorgeous bouquet of roses sent to her office ceremony. She loved them and had them in her apartment and cared for them for weeks.

I retired three years earlier than I normally would have. They called it an "Early Out". It did reduce somewhat the retirement annuity I would get. When talking with my colleagues prior to retirement, one said that if he were me, he would get out of here in a "New York minute". The fact that he was married and had several children (unlike me) and had to maximize his annuity certainly entered into his thinking. But as a result of what he said, I took advantage of the "early out" retirement provision. I never regretted it, but one could always have a larger annuity in his retirement years.

My 27 years of government service included three years in the army in WW II, two years with the Census Bureau and 22 years with the Department of the Army. As to what I did with my post-retirement, new-found time, more will come later. I will say at this point that, on the whole, I've been very pleased with the institution of retirement.

RODE TRAIN THROUGH COSTA RICAN RAIN FOREST - LIMÓN TO SAN JOSE

STOOD NEAR RIM OF DORMANT IRAZÚ VOLCANO, COSTA RICA - 1974

On my first vacation after retirement from my life's career Thelma and I went to a country I've heard a lot about as an inexpensive retirement location. That wasn't our primary reason for going. We just wanted to travel to a new country for us - one in which we would be comfortable traveling together as a couple.

We stayed in its capital, San Jose, for a few days. We took the "Tico Train" around the city. Tico is what the people of San Jose call themselves and the train is actually a motor driven sightseeing engine and car. It was fun. We also took in the large community market and the zoo and botanical gardens.

On another day, we were given a box lunch each and were to fly to the Caribbean coast, 70 or so miles east to Limón. Well, the day turned up cloudy with fog in the Limón area. After a long delay the flight was postponed until the next day. Being hungry again we decided to eat our lunches. At the airport the next day it was a go for Limón. We expected another box lunch, but we expected wrong. At our destination I had to eat, so I bought some cooked corn on the cob from a street vendor. It tasted so good. Of course, you are not supposed to eat local food unless prepared under sanitary conditions. I figured it was boiled and OK. I was wrong.

To return to San Jose from Limón we took a small gauge train which traversed the tropical rain forest. The variety of vegetation, bird-life, animal-sightings and scenery was close to overwhelming. It was an engrossing rail trip, one I don't guess we'll ever duplicate for interest. But after we got back and as I was getting into the taxi, Montezuma got his revenge. I felt plenty sick and responded to it. I was as sick as a dog for a couple of days. Thelma was wise to resist the temptation to eat local food and she mentioned it, darn it.

We were due to travel back to the States in two days and I wondered if I could make it. The transplanted Americans living in Costa Rica had a wonderful volunteer system of assisting travelers at the airport. They were very helpful in catering to our needs as best they could. I survived the trip home.

As to the Irazú Volcano, it was situated about a half-hour from our hotel in San Jose. We visited it a day or two prior to the Limón trip. I felt like doing the macho thing and going up close to the rim and peeking down. Well, it WAS a dormant volcano. Hadn't erupted in, what did they say, 500 years! But my curiosity was salved.

My first post-retirement vacation was a success, albeit with a blemish that taught me a lesson about foreign travel.

San Jose, Costa Rico – 'Tico Train'

ATE STEAK DINNER/WINE - $3, BUENOS AIRES, ARG. RESTAURANT - 1975

HAD LUNCH AT ARGENTINE ESTANCIA (CATTLE RANCH)

WALKED AMONGST INCA RUINS, MACHU PICCHU, PERU

Central America whetted our appetites, I suppose, for going further south in the Americas. So when we saw this trip to Brazil, Argentina and Peru, we signed on pronto. Souse America, here we come.

The Fred and Ginger movie "Flying Down to Rio" was definitely on our minds as we took off from Dulles International Airport outside Washington, DC and headed for Brazil. It was a nine hour flight just a little east of south to Rio.

We settled in a modern hotel some five miles or so by public transport west of Rio de Janiero proper - Gavea. We headed soon for the beach. We were forewarned not to leave any belongings unattended on the beach while in the water - they would be gone without a trace. No problemo - we either took turns dipping into the Atlantic on our own or we brought no extra accouterments at all.

Our next airport stop was Buenos Aires, Argentina. We stayed at an establishment near the harbor. I can remember watching with great interest the seaport activities taking place below.

But one evening we went to dine and soon realized we were in cattle country. That fact became apparent when we had a good steak dinner, with a salad and a bottle of wine (Argentinean) for the grand price of three dollars! The food was excellent and the price was doubly so.

A day or so later, we were transported to an estancia or Argentine cattle ranch. Besides some entertainment by gauchos, we were treated to some local dances and, of course, a good lunch.

But soon it was on to Peru to continue our circumnavigation of the southern continent. In Lima, we had a remarkable hotel, at least for Thelma and me. From the outside it looked like a normal building, but inside, all the floors were on balconies. One could step out his hotel door and look far down to the lobby floor. Interesting.

Eventually we flew to Cuzco high in the Andes. This small city is some two miles high. Bottles of oxygen are in the hotel lobbies to help people endure the extreme elevation. I know I felt uncomfortable but didn't need the oxygen. We went to Machu Picchu by train. Even though the well-preserved Inca site is high in the mountains, it actually has less elevation than Cuzco. One can only marvel at the site some five centuries old or so. It was only rediscovered early in the twentieth century.

As is well known, the stone masonry work of the early Peruvians was amazing - heavy stones which fit together so that a knife blade couldn't fit between them. We watched mountain climbers on an opposite peak do their daring feat.

What intrigued me in particular was seeing a bird soaring near another peak through my field glasses. I asked the guide about it and he confirmed for me that it was a giant Andes condor. Spying the big bird made the trip more complete than it already was.

After awhile we returned to our train to Cuzco using a small bus and a scary switchback road back down the mountain. What a day! What a week!

SAILED WASHINGTON, DC POTOMAC WATERS SOLO IN RENTED SAILBOAT -1975

Several blocks away from where we lived in Southwest, DC, were several marinas. Some were on a channel of the Potomac River and some were on the Anacostia River which joined the Potomac and formed Buzzard Point. It was here I rented a sailboat to try my hand at something new.

I had gone to the library to read up on sailboat maneuvering. It seemed like something I could do and fun to boot. My first problem, however, was getting out of the slip! The wind was blowing into the three-sided slip and I had a tough time getting out of there. The guy I rented from saw my predicament and helped me pull the boat out of its slip. Once out, things went smoothly.

I had taken several sailing trips. On another, I was tacking up the Anacostia and here comes a very large oil barge and tug. Sailboats have the right of way since they're less maneuverable, but I had no intention of testing out this rule of the waterways. I gave the barge wide berth until he had passed.

All in all though, it was very satisfying to use the angle of the sails in conjunction with the wind to cut your way through the water and go from point A to point B. I never felt proficient enough, however, to invite Thelma for a Sunday sail.

ATTENDED '76 OLYMPIC GAMES, MONTREAL, CANADA - 1976

TALKED WITH DON KARDONG, 4TH PLACE, '76 OLYMPIC MARATHON

One of my most favorite television watching activities of all is seeing the Olympic Games. Of course, like the US presidential elections and the attendant party conventions, it only happens every four years. Perhaps that is why the games are so engrossing. That reason, plus the fact that in these days I liked to jog and walk, gave Thelma and me a longing to see the Olympics this year taking place in Montreal, Canada.

I watched the newspapers months in advance to obtain information on obtaining tickets to particular events with dates and times. We got in touch with our Canadian friend from England whom we met on the Caribbean "Barefoot Cruise" three years earlier. She was living in Montreal. We just called her to get information on accommodations, but she was disappointed that we didn't want to stay with her and her friends. We didn't want to impose (but we did).

We opted for three events - the volleyball finals in the Forum where the famed Montreal Canadians ice hockey team normally held sway, an afternoon at the Olympic Stadium including the high jump finals and several running events including the marathon, and the closing ceremonies on the final day. The Forum was a city bus ride from Margaret's place. The finals had Poland up against the Russians. The contest was a "natural" battle and indeed it was. It took five sets to decide it and the Poles seemed to draw on deep reserves to beat a tired Russian team who hadn't lost a single set in the preliminary rounds! We got our money's worth on this one.

As to the stadium trip, we went by Metro. The stadium was beautiful with all of the nation's flags around the high, inside perimeter providing a very colorful decoration. The high jump was extra exciting with Dwight Stones, the American, losing out to the Canadian, Greg Joy, who was beaten in the final by the Polish lad Jacek Wszola in drizzly weather.

On our flight back to DC several days later, I spied a tall, thin fellow a row or two behind us. It turned out he was Don Kardong, who came in fourth in the olympic marathon. I had to speak to him which I did, interrupting another conversation he was having. This talk with Don Kardong was the capper to a memorable Olympic trip. Guess I had an added spring to my steps as I jogged my course the following weekend.

In the Stadium, 1976 Olympics, Montreal, Canada

STOPPED SMOKING AFTER 33 YEARS OF MODERATE INDULGENCE - 1978

I hadn't smoked when I was a kid, oh, maybe an experimental drag here and there. Then the army came along in 1942/43 and said "I Want You". While in the states and training for nine months, I still didn't buy or smoke any cigarettes. But then it came time for shipment overseas.

In the states, the PX's (GI stores) were well stocked and able to get more where those came from. But in the PX's in England, some of the goods were rationed - cigarettes and candy. Anyone who turned down his opportunity to purchase smokes or sweet stuff was a fool. Luckily I was able to trade my smokes for someone else's candy bars. I still remember my trading partner's name, Shannon Stewart. For a GI, he was old. We called him the 'old man'. He must have been in his mid-forties. Hell, he remembers when light bulbs had a pointy end!

Well, he finally left us just after the war ended in Europe in '45. Don't know why - maybe his age. But, this left me with no one to trade my cigarette ration for someone else's candy ration. At first the stuff piled up somewhat in my barracks bag. But then, and you know what's coming, I started to smoke them myself - for 33 years. I will say that at my heaviest period I smoked less than a half a pack a day. Later, I had reduced that to 6 or 8 butts a day.

But on the golf course one day in 1978, it just hit me - why am I doing this. Here I was jogging and smoking; the two are incompatible; I'm going to give up one or the other. That's the day I gave up the nicotine habit, cold.

As I recall, it wasn't easy for a month or so, but after that, I wondered why I hadn't done it sooner. And, of course, I'm so glad now that I did - so glad.

SIGNED COPIES OF MY BOOK AT AUTOGRAPH PARTY ABOARD HOUSEBOAT, DC - 1978

After retiring from formal employment, I had time on my hands. It actually was less time than I thought it would be, but there was some. I went to the library often, The Martin Luther King Library in DC, and started to investigate the history of Washington, DC, and more particularly, the Southwest quadrant of the city. This was my neighborhood since 1965.

I especially like to pour over old maps. I would ask for or pull down these large, bound, time-worn copies of DC maps through the years starting with the 1700's. Of course, checking the maps in closer detail would bring up questions that I would have to investigate further to satisfy my curiosity. I did keep a notebook of the information I uncovered and before I knew it, it was just about full.

Thelma saw it one day and told me I should write a book about the Southwest DC. I think in the back of my head I had this as an ultimate goal, but it took her comment to goad me into action.

With the notes assembled and organized together with photographs I had taken of various older structures in the new (redeveloped) Southwest, I eventually had my manuscript. It was entitled "South and West of the Capitol Dome". As a neophyte in the book writing business, I decided to take advantage of the services of a publishing firm which would obtain the copyright, publish and distribute for a fee, the so-called vanity press. In a matter of months I received the galley proofs and made my changes and corrections and sent it back. Some months later I had my 25 copies of the published book.

I think the biggest kick I got over the book publishing was seeing the book (and author) appear in the card catalogues of the local libraries, including the one at the Library of Congress.

We decided to have a book signing party. We took advantage of a houseboat from the local marina that was rented out for various parties and occasions. I'm not sure how we got the word out, but many of our friends were there. It turned out to be quite successful. Since the book had solely local appeal, its general acceptance was limited. I did set up a table at the local annual Southwest Festival held by the Southwest community in those days and made some sales through this avenue.

Autograph Party on Potomac River Houseboat

HIT, KNOCKED DOWN BY TURNING CAR, BUT OK, BRONX, NY - 1978

Thelma Martin's New York home, as mentioned previously, was in the Bronx. She was born on East 79th Street in Manhattan. Her father had died in the mid-thirties, but her mother lived on in the Bronx home on Paulding Avenue. More than occasionally, Thelma and I would go back home from Washington, DC - she to the Bronx, me to upper Manhattan (Inwood). I would drop her off and continue on to Manhattan and would reverse the procedure going back to DC.

Her mom died in the sixties, but Thelma continued to keep ownership of the private dwelling. She said she wanted to keep one foot in the Big Apple. The homeowners in the Bronx where the house was, resisted all attempts to have multiple apartment buildings in the neighborhood. It was a wonderful enclave somewhat near the famed Bronx Zoo. Even the nearby shops were delightful - German and Italian bakeries, green grocers, pork stores and other small but friendly specialty establishments.

After her mom died, we would spend more time there. She had the upper floor of the place remodeled and refurnished to her liking. Downstairs she had a renter and a caretaker.

At any rate, one day I was out jogging or walking and a driver turned into me as I was crossing with the light. It knocked me down and dazed me, but as it was a turn, he was not going very fast. Lucky for me! The guy apologized profusely. He said he had just gotten out of the hospital and was still groggy (doubtful). I obtained his name and address and went home and told Thelma. We immediately went to the Emergency Room of the local hospital (Albert Einstein Hospital) to get a medical check-up. They found nothing wrong. And that's the saga of the Bronx automobile knock down.

RODE HALF-TRACK VEHICLE IN SNOW TO OLD FAITHFUL GEYSER, WYO. - 1979

What possessed us to go to Wyoming in the dead of winter? The answer: It's contiguous to Montana! That explains it, but doesn't explain everything.

As you may surmise, I, and by proximity Thelma, am enthralled by natural phenomena. There was due to occur a total solar eclipse on February 26, 1979 in, among other places, central Montana. The eclipse would be the last TSE in the United States this century. Reason enough to go.

Two or three days after a very big snowstorm in Washington, DC, we hesitatingly left for the airport. The streets were still a mess and we wondered if it was this bad in DC, how bad might it be in Montana. But we fairly quickly got out to Bozeman, Mont., with stops in several cities along the way. The weather out west was gray also, but at least there were no big snow piles by the side of the road. We bused down to Big Sky Resort owned by NBC newscaster Chet Hundley.

Thelma and I opted for a cabin some distance from the main lodge. It was a beautiful choice. It took awhile, however, to figure out the little intricacies of getting a wood-burning fire to work properly. City boy - don't forget to open the damper! You learn by experience sometimes.

As a side trip, we bused down to Yellowstone National Park to take a half-track (Snow-Cat) trip into the park to see Old Faithful geyser put on its hourly blow. In the cold blue February sky, it was even more impressive than when I had seen it on a previous summer trip.

But, Monday, February 26, 1979 was approaching. On the day before, we had gotten the battle plan. About 500 of us were to pile into 15 buses at 2:00 AM. We certainly didn't want to be late for this bus trip! The plan was to let our meteorologist, Dr. Edward M. Brooks, direct us to a spot on the central eclipse line that was cloud free - no mean task. He had the help of aircraft reports and meteorological data.

We wound up on a lonely road near Lavina not far from the town of Roundup, Montana, pretty much in the center of the big state; buses to the left, people and telescopes/binoculars/cameras to the right facing the morning sun. And the sun was shining. There was a light, thin cloud cover, more like a haze. The ground was covered with snow no doubt contributing to the haze.

The temperature was about 25 degrees (F) at the moon's first contact with the sun's disk at about 8:20 AM, but very little wind. As the moon gradually covered the sun, some balloonists drifted by overhead. Some feared they would interfere with the total eclipse, but they were long gone by total time - about 9:27 AM. The temperature at mid-eclipse was a numbing 17 degrees (F), but the air was still and quiet. Of course, many excited people were witnessing the spectacle and their snow-muffled voices could be heard. Totality itself was, as it was in Sandbridge, Virginia in '70, an amazing sight to see. Because of the high thin clouds, the pearly corona around the moon/sun was subdued. But solar prominences were discernible. I'm a lucky man!

At arrival back at Big Sky Resort later in the afternoon, it was time for 'postmortems'. The scientists gave their slant on the morning's tremendous event. Dr. Brooks spoke about his personal fears and successes. But, of course, he was the hero, getting all those buses into position to witness one of nature's wonderful presentations.

Getting home by air was somewhat problematical with light snow falling at the Bozeman airport. But, we got off and were shunted to Pierre, South Dakota to avoid further snowstorms before arriving home to a sunny Washington, DC. Oh, we loved that trip.

'Old Faithful' in Wintertime, Yellowstone

RAN 10 MILE RACE WON BY BILL RODGERS, DC - 1979

I started playing golf when I worked for the Census Bureau. Golf is very much pursued in the DC/Maryland/Virginia area. I would usually play with my colleagues on a fairly routine basis. When I gained employment with the Army Department, the participation continued.

One day something dawned on me, however. Here I was setting the alarm clock for 5:30 or so on a Sunday morning so I could meet my buddies and get a good position on the 'wheel'. This was a devise which assured that the first to come would be the first to tee off. If you went at a more civilized hour, you would spend a lot of time waiting and ruin more than half your Sunday.

Also, since we usually played nine holes, you wouldn't get all that much exercise. So, instead, I started walking around the perimeter of the course which happened to be West Potomac Park or Hains Point in DC. Later, to improve my times, I started jogging. I was on my own schedule and I had myself a good healthy workout.

All the above is preliminary. Every year the District and other organizations sponsored the "Cherry Blossom Run" in the spring. It was 10 miles in length. I usually did ten kilometers or about six miles, so if I wanted to enter I would have to train some at the new distance, which I did. The race attracted world-class runners one of which was Bill Rodgers, a Massachusetts marathoner. The race takes place on virtually the same course I habitually run on Sunday mornings. It also wound around some of the famous Japanese cherry trees which blossomed at this time. It was beautiful.

At any rate, the favorite, Rodgers won the race. I was happy to have finished the race in a respectable time for an amateur, though way down the list of finishers. But I can truthfully say that the famous runner, Bill Rodgers, beat me fair and square in a 10 mile footrace!

ASTONISHED AT VIEW OF TAJ MAHAL FROM ENTRANCE AREA GATE, AGRA, INDIA - 1980

RODE ELEPHANT-BACK TO SEE AMBER PALACE, JAIPUR, INDIA

USED MARBLE BATHROOM IN JAIPUR, INDIA HOTEL

SWAM IN ARABIAN SEA OFF INDIAN COAST, GOA

I suppose we took the trip of a lifetime when Thelma and I decided to fly to India via London and Rome. We went with a group - a group specializing in total solar eclipse trips around the world. It wasn't inexpensive, but when you're young and in your prime earning years you do things like this. If we saw this eclipse, it would have been my third - and that's the way it turned out.

After landing in New Delhi and settling into our hotel, we spent a day or so sightseeing around the city as a group. We saw old forts, grand government promenades, mosques and parks inhabited by monkeys. (Ladies, watch your handbags). Indian temperatures were fine in February. Earlier it would be colder, later it would be hot until the monsoon season arrives in June. Later we were bused to Agra to see, perhaps, the most gorgeous building in the world - the Taj Mahal. The first glimpse of it from the entrance gate area took my breath away. Later we would be impressed anew as we walked into it and through it, but that first glance really knocked me for a loop.

On the way to Jaipur, we stopped to see the Amber Palace. But it was on top of a high hill. To get there, four of us rode on an elephant's back - what else would be appropriate? Thelma and I were on the animal's right flank and two other members of the group, whom we hadn't met, were on the left. The lady of the other couple was quietly singing something to which I responded that she had a good voice. Her partner chimed in that she better, she's an opera singer! I think they said her name was Dorothy (I didn't get the last name), but I did see it listed in connection with music somewhere. The elephant trip was delightful.

In Jaipur, called the Pink City because of the coloration of its stones, we made the usual tour of this unusual city. India, although having some of the worst poverty anyone is likely to ever see, is, nevertheless, like a giant circus. Steers in the streets, camels along the roads, peacocks on the grassy plots, monkeys and snake-charmers in the parks, women in their colorful saris and processions of elephants at the tourist venues, all under a big, orange-yellow sun with the ubiquitous colorful birds thrown into the mix. Simply unbelievably fascinating.

Then, back at the hotel, one could attend to his or her ablutions in a marble bathroom - and I don't mean faux.

Then it was south to Bombay (now Mumbai) and Mahatma Gandhi's former residence in the city. Two days later we flew to Goa, the former Portuguese enclave on the west coast. We stayed at a fine hotel (but no marble bathroom) on the coast of the Arabian Sea. The hotel was a training facility for future native hotel workers. The facilities were excellent, but quite a few of the group had "Delhi Belly" - no joke if you are one of the sufferers. I remember one older guy, while we were floating around in the Arabian Sea, telling me that the waters were positively therapeutic after what he had been through on the trip down from New Delhi. He was so thankful to be feeling better. My companion, Thelma, was a stickler for following all the literature which warned us to drink only bottled water and not to eat uncooked foods. Luckily, I followed her advice this time.

And on the final full day of the trip we got into position to catch the total solar eclipse. It started at 2:15 PM local time with the sun about 40 degrees above the western horizon. The sight during totality was magnificent. Even the local folks were enthralled by the event. It was an amazing end to an amazing trip in an amazing country. Memories would be long after this one.

Elephant Ride to Amber Fort, India

WON HONORABLE MENTION IN SOUTHWEST, DC PHOTOGRAPHY CONTEST - 1980

Thelma Martin was the prime mover in establishing a Southwest Photography Group. We held regular meetings holding discussions on photography, cameras, picture taking locales and equipment. We invited guests to speak and provide us with some expertise in picture taking.

Once a year we held a photography contest in which anyone could submit their photos for a modest prize. There was even a special prize for school kids to compete with other children. We displayed the photos in the contest in various local sites; one time in a waterfront motel, another time in the branch library and a third time in the lobby of the headquarters of the Disabled American Veterans.

For awhile, the Group was doing quite well in the area. We went so far as to put out a newsletter providing information to the amateur photographers.

I tried my hand at submitting a photo. The so-called Tall Ships made an appearance in the DC area. I took one photo of the Norwegian ship "Christian Radich" while it was tied up at dockside. The deckhands were all forward on the ship in their orange and yellow slickers. Beneath them, under the bow, was the ships figurehead, a pretty woman dressed in blue. I entitled the photo "The Lady and the Gentlemen". I thought the juxtaposition of the gray ship, colorfully garbed sailors and the lady on the bow with her blue dress seemingly flowing in the breeze made an interesting photo. It did take honorable mention which I was happy to receive. And that was the beginning (and the end) of my pursuit of a career in award winning photography.

SWAM FROM BLACK PEBBLE BEACH, BLACK SEA, YALTA, USSR - 1981

MARVELED AT ART WORKS, HERMITAGE, LENINGRAD (ST. PETERSBURG)

RODE HYDROFOIL TO PETRODVORETS, CZAR'S SUMMER PALACE, LENINGRAD

CRUISED CRYSTAL CLEAR LAKE BAIKAL, SIBERIA, USSR

WAITED FOR TRANS-SIBERIAN TRAIN TO PASS, BRATSK, SIBERIA

By this time, total solar eclipse watching was an activity I had to pursue. I was well rewarded with TSE viewings in Virginia (1970), Montana (1979) and India (1980). I was checking the books to see where in the world the next one would be. It gave us pause. It was to be in Siberia, USSR on July 31, 1981. It gave Thelma so much pause, she decided not to go - not only because of the distance involved but because of the country itself. As a fellow Cold War Warrior, she didn't feel up to taking a trip such as this one. I, on the other hand, was curious - curious about the eclipse, about how it would be handled in the USSR and about this rogue country I had been reading about all my life. I decided to go without Thelma.

I flew to Montreal and met up with the tour group I would be traveling with. We took off at 7:15 PM in a Russian Alushia 62, using all of the runway to get airborne. Supper was 3 1/2 hours later and sunrise was 4 1/2 hours after takeoff. We were traveling the great circle route over Greenland and Iceland, not that I saw anything of these areas. The complete trip was seven hours in length (we crossed eight time zones) and we arrived in Moscow at 10:15 AM the next morning.

We were met by our Russian tourist leader, Tanya - a very efficient and capable young lady - who assisted us through customs and currency exchange. Then, after an airport lunch, we connected to our next flight to Yalta at another Moscow airport. We arrived late at night so this was one long day.

At Yalta on the Black Sea, we arrived so late we were put in a small hotel instead of the more modern Yalta Hotel. But the Oriander Hotel had a better location, closer to Yalta and on the "boardwalk" near the sea. I put boardwalk in quotes because it was actually a paved street from which vehicular traffic was barred. I enjoyed the day we went to the black pebble beach. Wooden walks were put over the big pebbles to facilitate walking and reclining. Tanya was with us and I grew to like the girl. The swimming was fun and refreshing.

After numerous side trips in Yalta, we went to the site of the Yalta Conference in 1945 between FDR, Stalin and Churchill. Very interesting. I took pictures and compared them, after I returned home, with photos of the conference taken in '45.

Our next flight was to St. Petersburg, then Leningrad. We landed in a thunder storm with the lightning visible in the clouds below us in the twilight. There were many sights in the city built originally by Peter the Great. The world famous Hermitage was probably the most engaging. The building, almost akin to a warehouse inside, housed some of the most valuable and treasured artwork on the planet. Crowds of people were shuffling through the corridors and rooms. The paintings and statues were a once in a lifetime visitation.

In Leningrad, we climbed aboard a, maybe, fifty foot hydrofoil vessel, the kind that has its hull ride above the water on foils or blades when it attains a good speed. Our destination was 20 or so miles west on an arm of the Gulf of Finland - Petrodvorets, the czar's summer residence. It was a beautiful spot containing many gravity-fed water fountains and overlooking the gulf. Some fountains would mysteriously and whimsically spurt at a time you would least expect it.

We flew back down to Moscow to catch another flight to Irkutsk, north of Mongolia. The wait at Moscow was relieved by the numerous stands selling ice cream. As it turned out, we stopped short of Irkutsk because of fog at their airport. We touched down in Bratsk which we were scheduled to visit after our stay in Irkutsk. But we did finally make it to Irkutsk, took the obligatory city tour, walked along the Ankara River (its waters destined to wind up in the Arctic Ocean), and met some English tourists who asked us if we had heard about the wedding between Prince Charles and Diana that day. We hadn't.

We bused east along the Ankara to its inception at Lake Baikal. The Ankara is the only river flowing out of Lake Baikal; 360 rivers flow into the lake. We took another hydrofoil craft onto the lake itself which is exceptionally clear. It contains fauna seen nowhere else on earth. The lake is a world treasure.

We finally made it back to Bratsk where we had to arise at 4:00 AM to catch a river boat to the site the Russians had established to view the total solar eclipse. I successfully witnessed my fourth TSE, the third in as many years. It was a beautiful experience, especially considering the setting.

Back at Bratsk later, we bused through the town established as a result of a large dam construction, which we toured. During the bus ride at one point we had to wait as a Trans-Siberian train passed by.

Then, it was back to Moscow, the tour of the city and the Kremlin, shopping at GUM (the government Department Store), witnessing the changing of the guard at Lenin's Tomb on Red Square, attending the farewell dinner provided, I think, by the Russian tourist agency, Intourist. What a trip! And we still had the great circle flight home to Montreal. This time I did catch a glimpse of the southern tip of Greenland.

INSTIGATED ACTION ON OUR FAMILY'S GENEALOGY & REUNIONS - 1982

Living in Washington, DC, I was fairly isolated from most of my family members a great deal. My New York home was gone by this time, my mother having passed on in '56, my father in '65, my sister in '71 and my brother living in Florida with his wife and two of his three children. I had cousins and second cousins in Pennsylvania, New Jersey and New York State. But I was confused as to the what, who, where, why and when of the clan. I'm talking here of my mother's side of the family; my father was the only member, as far as I know, to come to the new world (from England).

With time and curiosity, I drafted a chart similar to a company organizational chart, and, starting from my mother's parents, put in their children, grandchildren (like me), great grandchildren and so on. If nothing else, this uncovered the extent of my ignorance.

So I sent out forms to all family member households asking for data on names, dates of birth, dates of marriage and dates of death where applicable. I traveled to London primarily to delve into genealogical information about my father and his parents. The day in London I received copies of my English father's birth certificate and my paternal grandparents marriage and birth certificates was a very happy day for me.

After corresponding with various city and state authorities and the federal Census Bureau, I was able to put together a family album entitled "The Meier Family in the USA" (my mother's folks came from Germany). Old and new photographs were used to illustrate the album. Then, in 1984, I bought my first personal computer and was amazed to discover the software which permitted much easier manipulation of the mounting data.

I then initiated requests to hold family reunions in various households which received encouraging responses. Our reunions, well attended although not large, were held in New York State (2), in Pennsylvania (2) and in southern New Jersey.

So, on the whole, I was quite pleased with myself in accomplishing what I did for the family and, I think, the efforts were well received by family members. It gives a sense of family cohesion, especially for the younger folks.

WAS CLOSE TO QUEEN ELIZABETH II, LINCOLN MEMORIAL, DC - 1982

It was in the newspapers and on TV; Queen Elizabeth II of Britain was visiting the US, the District and President Reagan. On her schedule was a visit to the Lincoln Memorial. Since that was generally in my walking and jogging zone, I decided to amble on up there.

It was a fine spring day or possibly an early summer one. At any rate, it was a pleasant day. I went up the steps in front of the memorial I guess more than half way to mingle with other folks wanting to see the monarch. There was a good crowd there, but not overly so and they were well behaved. I wasn't aware of any security personnel, although I'm sure there had to be some.

The queen had already been up the stairs and I'm sure viewed the statue of the giant, seated Abraham Lincoln made of pristine white marble. The memorial, with the statue and the Lincoln quotations around three sides of the columned building, was a humbling experience for me and probably for millions of people throughout the years. I'm sure it must have been for Queen Elizabeth also.

But finally she completed her visitation and began to descend the massive stairway. Her pathway down was roped off, but as she passed me I saw the serene lady clearly. As usual, her smile and hand gestures were conservative and subdued - every inch those of a royal sovereign. It was a memory which can be classified in my book as one of my lifetime's unusual events.

ACTED AS CAT-HANDLER WHEN OUR ABYSINIAN LORD SANDPUR (SANDY) TOOK RIBBONS WHEN ENTERED IN DC REGIONAL CAT SHOWS - 1982

Thelma and I used to go to cat shows held in the area. She got to talking with one lady who was showing her Abyssinian cat. This is a breed which may, they are not sure, have been the pets of the early Egyptians. The breed is almost pure beige with some white around the neck. Their energy is high and their disposition is excellent.

The lady talked us into buying one - she was raising them. In deference to his color, we called him Sandy. Since he was a pure bred Abyssinian, we decided to try our hand at showing him at various cat shows around the area. The name "Sandy" wasn't good enough for the name of a show cat and since he was born in the "Sokitume" cat-breeder facility, we called him "Lord Sandpur of Sokitume".

Thelma thought it might be better if I did the handling of the cat at the shows. I was kind of proud to do the honors - keeping track of announcements about bringing the particular breed and class to the judging cages, carrying the cat to the judging tables, overseeing the judging and retrieving cat (and ribbons) at the conclusion of the judging. In a crowded show, you had to be careful. More than once the cry went up "cat loose - watch the doors".

But Sandy did fine. He garnered quite a few ribbons and rosettes in his show time career (a few years). Needless to say, his parents were mighty proud of the feline.

Lord Sandpur (Sandy) – Show Cat Winner

PADDLED RENTED CANOE THROUGH OKEFENOKEE SWAMP, GA. - 1983

As one ages, one wants to get more for his vacation buck. One way to get this is to join an Elderhostel group. This is an outfit from Boston which arranges accommodations and educational activities for groups of older people, usually at a university or nature center. There are no strict requirements, such as homework to perform or tests to take. The lectures and study are up to the individuals to absorb on their own. The lodgings are comfortable but not extravagant. Stays are usually for five days or so.

I took my first Elderhostel trip in Rhode Island to study woodland flora and fauna. A canoe trip was on that agenda. The second was to Georgia to learn more about Mark Twain and his works. I took a side trip on my own to the Okefenokee Swamp. I rented a canoe and glided amongst the lily pads and moss beds, flowering bushes and tall trees, alligators and eagles. The water was still and black which reflected images like a mirror. The darkness of the water is caused by the tannin from trees. I got back that old sense of accomplishment again after returning to home base.

Other Elderhostel trips included one to West Virginia high in the mountains and others to Prescott, Arizona, eastern Kentucky and Chincoteaque, Virginia, both of the latter with my wife Lu and, finally, to Smith Mountain Lake in western Virginia. Every trip was exceedingly interesting and a minor adventure. I recommend this way of seeing the world as a relatively inexpensive and rewarding vacation activity. The Elderhostel catalog is a half inch thick and packed with an almost bewildering array of places to spend a week. One could usually drive to the site, at least for the stays in nearby states.

Okefenokee Swamp, Georgia Canoe Trip

WITNESSED PART OF TRIAL, OLD BAILEY, LONDON - 1984

JOGGED THROUGH STREETS AND REGENT'S PARK OF LONDON

STOOD ASTRIDE 0 DEGREE LONGITUDE, GREENWICH, ENGLAND

London - I had been there during WW II, it was the birthplace of my father and it rivaled in size and complexity my home town of New York City. So as I delved into genealogy more intensely, it was apparent that I had to go to the big city on the Thames.

When English customs asked me what the purpose of my visit was, I told them genealogy and it seemed to please the customs officer. I flew in to Heathrow Airport, took the tube into town at a stop surprisingly close to my hotel (The President, I believe). I was surprised at the many points of interest which were within walking distance of this walker.

There was the British Museum (I wanted to view the Rosetta Stone in particular), then there was Berkeley Square (I heard no nightingale sing, however, but I hummed that song and 'A Foggy Day' all that morning), there was the Marylebone area where my father's parents lived when he was born 98 years earlier and there was the public records office enabling an amateur genealogist like me to obtain copies of my father's and paternal grandfather's birth certificates and marriage certificate. There was also Regent's Park where I did a little jogging to keep in shape.

And while walking along on Strand Street in east London, I passed the Royal Courts. While in the building, I just continued walking and looking, half expecting to be stopped somewhere along the ornate corridors, but I wasn't. I went up one flight of stairs and into one court in session. There were three white- wigged justices and, of course, the tables of solicitors, defendants and plaintiffs. The witness box, like the judges' bench was elevated. But we spectators were the highest of all - we were in a balcony overseeing the trial.

I wasn't there long enough to garner many details, but it was a semi-thrill to witness an English trial, if ever so briefly. It was interesting to notice how similar our court system is, although certainly not in every detail. So much for "Old Bailey". It did bring to mind those many movies and TV shows of English trials, and Mr. Rumpole too!

A day or two later I hopped a river boat to ride the Thames east to Greenwich. Along the way, we saw the massive gates being erected on the river. Periodically, a North Sea storm would drive tons of water up the Thames estuary causing devastating flood damage. These gates would be moved into place beforehand to foil the inundation. But, we soon tied up in Greenwich. This is the town renowned for being the initial line, the zero longitude of the world. There was an old observatory there, but newer technology has rendered it obsolete. Instead, an interesting museum can be visited with a fine collection of old timepieces. But the major focus of the location was the demarcation in the sidewalk of the zero degree line of longitude. One can stand with one foot in the Eastern Hemisphere and the other in the Western Hemisphere. East <u>does</u> meet West!

East meet West, Greenwich, England

SAT IN US SUPREME COURT JUSTICE'S CHAIR, DC - 1985

My girlfriend had many friends, but particularly she had the ones she went to school with in Berkeley, California. One of them had a daughter who pursued a professional ballet career. More on her later. Another, whose first name was Jane, married a man who became a judge in the New York judicial system. His name was Newman - Peter, I think. This couple had two daughters and a son.

The older daughter, Lisa, went into medicine and became a surgeon operating in the Boston area. The second oldest, Debra, studied law and became a lawyer. The last I heard, she followed her father and became a judge. Finally, there was the boy, also Peter. He was in his last term as an undergraduate at Georgetown University.

The whole family would come down from New York where they lived to attend to business and to see Peter. Debra was attending law school at GU also. Thelma often called Debra her "play daughter". Debra would be pouring over her law books in Thelma's kitchen one evening to prepare for some new test or something.

But back to young Peter. He had spent a summer as a US House of Representative page boy. I'm sure his father greased the slides on that one. He invited Thelma and me over to his small apartment on the hill one day. He made spaghetti for us which was nice of him, although I didn't much care for the taste somehow.

But on his last summer semester, he became a law assistant to one of the US Supreme Court justices. I don't recall that he was assisting any one in particular, but it could have been. He invited me over to the court to show me around. Needless to say, I was tickled pink. Since the court was not in session, he took me to the exalted courtroom itself where the nine justices heard arguments for the nation's most important cases. Thus it was that I sat in one of the justices high-backed and comfortable chairs for all of thirty seconds. Cool.

A few months later the Newmans invited Thelma and me to young Peter's graduation ceremony at Georgetown University and we were glad they did.

The Ward's (Fred, Richard, Minnie, William, Marian)

CALLED UP WARD FAMILY PICTURE, STATUE OF LIBERTY MUSEUM, NY - 1986

Nineteen-eighty-six was the year the Statue of Liberty in New York harbor became 100 years old. In anticipation of this milestone, the innards of the statue were renovated, and, it turned out, not a moment too soon. The corrosion had reached a critical level.

But also in anticipation of the milestone year, a great celebration was planned. There were to be speakers - President Reagan was there - fireboat water displays, visits by old-time sailing vessels and, of course, music and fireworks. Seems as if no one was going to forget the welcoming lady with the torch and tablet. In addition, most of the larger commercial concerns in the country donated funds.

The Kodak Company devised a plan to display, in the Statue's Museum, family pictures sent in by people throughout the country. The scheme was to apply a five digit number to the family photo which could be called up at a computer station in the museum. So, I submitted a photo of the Ward family - all five members - taken 32 years earlier and I eventually received my five digit number - 71473.

Naturally, we had to check it out. The next time Thelma and I went to NYC, we hopped the ferry at Battery Park as soon as we could and glided out to Liberty Island in the harbor. We old-timers remember the Statue of Liberty Island as Bedloes Island. Believe it or not, even though both of us were native New Yorkers, we had never been to the statue. The line to get into the statue was quite long, so I convinced Thelma to accompany me to the museum. We found the 'magic' computer, typed in '71473', and lo and behold, there was our Ward family photograph on the big screen television in full view of everybody. Love it!

Unfortunately, I've never been back to observe if the thing still works or even if they still have the protocol! I've got to do it one of these months. I've got to. I'm not getting any younger.

WALKED ACROSS UPPER CROSSING, TOWER BRIDGE, LONDON, ENGLAND - 1987

I'm not sure what the primary motivation was, but Thelma and I went to London this year. It was mostly a sight-seeing adventure no doubt. Two things I remember distinctly.

The day we picked to investigate the Tower of London and the nearby Tower Bridge across the Thames, often thought of by Americans as London Bridge, was a poor day from a weather standpoint. As a matter of fact, there were gales in southern England which caused significant property damage. In London, it was just somewhat windy and rainy.

We started to walk across the bridge on the main level when some gusts almost knocked us down. Thelma said she would not continue. I did, maybe halfway, and then retreated. But we got to the tower where the lifts (elevators) were and went up to the upper crossing. This part of the bridge was protected from the winds. We proceeded across the upper crossing. The views up and down the Thames were magnificent. On the south shore (Southwark), a warship was tied up. On the London side, one could see the Tower of London, St Paul's Cathedral, the aforementioned London Bridge and other Thames crossings. It was an engrossing sight. The downstream view showed a lot of waterfront activity and construction.

We didn't linger long in the Tower of London, but Thelma had to see the famed Beefeaters, the legendary Tower guards. She was enthralled by their colorful uniforms.

One evening we had tickets for the long-running musical 'Cats'. The fact that we were cat owners ourselves had nothing to do with our decision. Not! Anyway, we had dinner at a Chinese restaurant not far from Trafalgar Square. It was very good, but we expected quicker service. As a result, we got to the theatre after the opening. As a consequence, we weren't allowed into the theatre proper until the end of the first act. We could see what was happening on a closed circuit telly in the lobby. Getting to our balcony seats after the first act was a chore. We had to sidle pass so many people to get to our central, interior seats. We were happy to finally sit.

The musical was so good, as all plays with lyrics by Andrew Lloyd Weber invariably are. The hit number, I suppose, is 'Memories' and it brought tears to my eyes. I never forgot that rendition or the song - it was so, well, so haunting.

London's Tower Bridge, Tower of London to left

WAS JURY FOREMAN IN DC MURDER TRIAL - 1987

The District of Columbia certainly has its share of crime, perhaps to an over-publicized degree. I first came to the District at age 27 in 1950. As of this year, I've been called for jury duty in this jurisdiction three times or once every twelve years on average. Doesn't seem to be an outrageous ratio.

But I did serve this year. As probably happens in most jurisdictions, you have to show up to enter a pool of prospective jurors. Sometimes you're released to report again and other times you're called to report to a courtroom. Sometimes you're dismissed after twelve jurors (and two alternates) have been selected. On a previous trial, I was selected as an alternate, heard the whole trial and then, since all twelve saw the trial to completion prior to deliberation, was dismissed. I was very interested in finding out how the jury voted, but I had to do it on my own.

But on this day and trial, I vaulted every hurdle - I became one of the twelve jurors on a murder trial. In general, the defendant, a professional baker, was accused of shooting someone to death following an Independence Day celebration. The government's lawyers were good, but the defendant had a flamboyant, silver-tongued attorney who had a reputation in the community for his oratorical ability.

The trial lasted about a week. We were continually admonished to remain silent on the case until its conclusion. I wanted to tell Thelma some of the details, but I held my tongue.

In the jury deliberation room, we voted on a foreperson. After someone nominated me, I suggested another person. Maybe my age (64) and conservative demeanor convinced the majority to look in my direction but, at any rate, I was voted in as foreman.

I wanted to hear everyone's expressed thoughts about the case, so I made a point of drawing out every juror. One of the defense's points was that the accused had his back to a closed door behind him and had to act in self-defense. I thought this point was weak as I demonstrated how I, with my back to the jury door, could feel for the knob and get out the door behind me. But the preponderance of evidence seemed to be in the defendant's favor. With two or three juror votes, we voted to acquit.

It's a rather scary proposition to pass judgment on a series of events you hear second or third hand on a terribly important event. But, I didn't volunteer for this duty - I was drafted and I did the best that I knew how. This type of thinking permitted a better night's sleep at the end of the day. One thing I'm aware of - I will still be thinking about it twenty-odd years later as I write this.

PLIED KLONGS (CANALS) IN BANGKOK,
THAILAND - 1988

SIPPED SINGAPORE SLING IN RAFFLES
HOTEL BAR, SINGAPORE

BOARDED GOLDEN ODYSSEY IN SINGAPORE
FOR TRIP ON JAVA SEA TO BALI

CHATTED WITH ASTRONAUT MIKE COLLINS
ON TENDER TO BALI

SAW TOTAL SOLAR ECLIPSE FROM
GOLDEN ODYSSEY, CELEBES SEA

CLIMBED PAGODA IN GUANGZHOU
(CANTON), CHINA

CROSSED HONG KONG HARBOR FROM
KOWLOON ON STAR FERRY

SAW LINER QUEEN ELIZABETH FROM
VICTORIA PEAK, HONG KONG

BREAKFASTED OFF WAIKIKI BEACH,
ROYAL HAWAIIAN HOTEL

There's another total solar eclipse due this year, but in Southeast Asia? So be it. Thelma and I have the bug - we can't resist and it's hopeless to try.

I suppose one could question a person's sanity to fly halfway around the world to see an event he's already seen four times, but that's exactly what Thelma and I did. But the total solar eclipse, as spectacular an event as nature has to offer, wasn't the sole highlight of the trip.

Scientific Expeditions (under World of Oz) set up this magnificent tour; a flight to Hong Kong after a refueling in Japan; a couple of days in Hong Kong and then a flight to Bangkok, Thailand; after two/three days in the klong (canal) city, we would fly to Singapore and after a day, we would take the "Golden Odyssey" (that name alone would make the trip a success!) of the Royal Cruise Lines, Ltd. to Hong Kong a second time via Bali in Indonesia, Sandakan in Malaysia, Manila in the Philippines and Guangzhou (Canton in the old days) in the PRC (China). And what about viewing the total eclipse? That little feat would be accomplished on the western Celebes Sea east of Borneo. I would readily say that this trip would be hard to top for sheer exotic variety.

There was plying the klongs of Bangkok in our wooden launches; the meal on board the Cathay Pacific Airline flight to Singapore preceded by hot hand towels and appetizers; a Singapore Sling served in the famed Raffles Hotel bar in Singapore; cruising the Java Sea on the "Golden Odyssey" with the next port-of-call - Bali; making light conversation with Michael Collins 19 years after his orbits of the moon while waiting for Neil Armstrong to make his "one small step" statement; a perfect total solar eclipse while floating in the Celebes Sea; watching tamed orangutan youngsters being trained to be reintroduced into the jungles of Borneo; enjoying the agility of bamboo dancers in a Manila musical presentation; climbing a multi-storied pagoda to view Canton from on high; the Star Ferry ride from Kowloon to Hong Kong Island; viewing the docked "Queen Elizabeth" from high on Victoria Peak in Hong Kong; having breakfast at the Royal Hawaiian Hotel on Waikiki Beach (Thelma had to say hello to aging actor Tony Curtis who was on the beach painting a picture); and last but not least, being treated to an aquatic presentation with dolphins, seals and penguins on the north shore of Oahu in Hawaii.

Needless to say, this trip flashed by very quickly. As to details of the eclipse on March 18, 1988, Friday dawned brightly. We got an open spot on the Bridge Deck of the "Golden Odyssey" overlooking the aft pool. I had set up my trusty thermometer in a shady place and at 8:42 AM it read 82 degrees F. As time slipped by the temperature rose to 88 and stayed there till 9:07 when it started to fall slowly. At mid-eclipse at 9:52, the thermometer read 80. The eclipse itself was unbelievably beautiful -- a big black hole in the sky surrounded closely by a pearly corona, with tiny prominences of fiery red poking out from the black moon disk. We humans are blessed in many ways, but to be alive at a time when our satellite's size and distance from the sun allows it to exactly cover our life-giving star periodically, stretches credulity. The temperature rose back to 88 degrees by eclipse end at 11:10 AM.

We beat the odds again - a great spectacle. Later, it was postmortem time as the tour group heard the professionals rehash the day's event. Others showed us their camcorder results. Of course, we all congratulated everybody connected with getting us to that spot on earth at that one particular moment. Incidentally, we were very near the equator on very nearly the spring equinox, meaning the sun was directly over us at local noon. Our shadows were at their minimum!

This was about the midpoint of our trip. From now on it was downhill, but what a downhill - Manila, Canton, Hong Kong and Honolulu. It was a never to be forgotten journey. Thelma and I enjoyed it immensely and have the film to prove it - if we ever had the feeling that the trip was just a dream.

Chinese Guide in Guangzhou (Canton)

TOOK FERRY TRIP FROM SPAIN PASSED
GIBRALTAR TO AFRICA - 1989

This year we opted for Europe again. No eclipse, just wanted to gain a new experience by renting an apartment for a week in Spain on the Mediterranean coast on the Costa Del Sol. When Thelma heard about my plan she said that she wasn't going to be cooking on her vacation abroad. I agreed. But between going out to eat, eating convenience foods and me helping out with the kitchen chores, we got through the adventure without a problem.

The hotel/apartment complex was great. It had a gigantic pool complex composed of several pools, slides (long ones) and a diving facility. The complex also had gardens and walkways and some shops. One of the shops was a food mini-market - very handy.

We arrived in Spain via Brussels, Belgium and then Madrid where we stayed a day or two. After Madrid we flew to Málaga before busing 25 miles or so west to Torremolinos where our apartment was. Even though this was March, the swimming was fine, though it wasn't hot. Thelma and I had our choice of the pool complex or the Mediterranean. Seemed as if there were more topless girls on the beach, but I swam in the pools also.

We decided to take a side trip to Morocco. We were bused to Algeciras near Gibraltar where we boarded the ferry, a really big boat, and took off for the African coast across the Straits of Gibraltar. We got a good view of the famous rock on the port side as we passed it by.

We stayed overnight in a pretty Moroccan hotel. We visited the local Casbah, saw snake trainers, had a camel ride and (Thelma) bought some rugs - just your typical American tourist activities! We were back in Torremolinos the next evening. By the way, there was an excellent suburban train service between Torremolinos and the big town of Málaga. We took advantage of it to visit the town's department stores and do some rubber-necking. We really did have a fine vacation - Thelma was glad I persisted in my original plan.

Camel Ride, Morocco

Tour Group Supper, Costa del Sol, Spain

VIEWED GRAND CANYON IN DISAPPEARING DAYTIME FOG, AZ - 1990

Thelma Martin was back to work after her retirement. I think she was that kind of person who just likes the discipline of scheduled activity. At any rate, I decided to go west this year on my own, but on a less expensive journey. I decided to take an Elderhostel trip to Arizona.

The hotel we would be staying at was in Prescott in northwest Arizona. The program would involve a side trip to the Grand Canyon which I had never seen and didn't propose to grow too old without seeing - the Canyon or, for that matter, Yellowstone prior to my visits there. So I dusted off my bags and Western hat and took off to the airport and eventually wound up in Phoenix.

I had to bus to Prescott to meet up with the other Elderhostel members. We had several side trips in the area, but then it was time for the big ditch. I couldn't wait.

We arrived at the Canyon rather early in the morning. The sun was just beginning to burn off the wisps and spires and streaks of fog. I think it added to the vista, giving the Canyon an added sense of depth. All I know is that I was really touched by the vast scene in front of me. I teared up. So vast, so gorgeous, so isolated, so unbelievable. Abe Burrows, the old time playwright/director/comedian once said this about the Natural Bridge in Virginia – "What's to prevent it?" True enough, but the very fact that it <u>is</u> there puts it in the miraculous category.

Within a half an hour, the fog had disappeared and the Canyon was laid out in front of us in all its myriad shapes and colors. Hey, this is as great as a total solar eclipse!

But soon it was back to Prescott, back to Phoenix (almost missed the bus though), and back to DC and home. Yes, I can chalk up another fine visit to another fine place on this old earth of ours.

SAW THELMA'S FRIEND & LEAD BALLERINA VIRGINIA JOHNSON, "GIZELLE", ROYAL OPERA HOUSE, LONDON - 1992

My girlfriend Thelma's old school chum from Berkeley, California had a daughter who was a professional ballet dancer. Virginia Johnson had performed in ballet productions around the country. But Thelma got word that Virginia would be given the lead in "Gizelle" to be performed at the Royal Opera House in London. I suppose the Johnson's were thrilled - I know Thelma was. Thelma treated me to a round-trip ticket to Great Britain to see her friend's daughter perform. Of course, I accepted with gratitude.

We stayed at a fine hotel not far from the opera house. Virginia herself was entitled to a nearby flat, as they call it here, to which we were invited to visit with her and her family. It was a very large and nice apartment. On the evening of the performance, we showed up at our assigned seats with her parents seated not far away.

I'll be frank. I'm not especially caught up in the ballet scene, but will admit to enjoying the beauty and spectacle of the show that evening. I could tell that Thelma was overjoyed. After the show we went around inside the rear of the theater to congratulate Virginia in her dressing room on her stellar performance. I'm sure the Brits in the audience were equally enchanted with her part in the production judging from the applause and curtain calls.

A day or two later there was a reception held for her at the British Embassy guest house. Thelma and I were invited. There we were, the two of us, hobnobbing with all sorts of VIPs. I was talking with a Member of Parliament (or MP as we say). Our mutual discussion points were my English father and his trip to the States recently. All very interesting.

But the time soon came when we had to return to our hotel, airport, airplane seats and home. Thanks Thelma for a wonderful interlude. It will be everlastingly remembered.

Ballerina Virginia Johnson with Thelma

SAW UP CLOSE ENORMOUS STATUE "CHRIST THE REDEEMER" OVERLOOKING RIO DE JANEIRO, BRAZIL - 1992

RODE SUGAR LOAF AERIAL CAR, RIO

SWAM FROM COPACABANA BEACH, RIO WITH ECLIPSE-CHASING BUDDIES BRAZIL

SPRAYED BY MIST BENEATH IGUASU FALLS, BRAZIL/ARGENTINA

WATCHED PARTIAL SOLAR ECLIPSE AT SUNRISE NEAR PUNTA DEL ESTE, URUGUAY

SAW TANGO SHOW, BUENOS AIRES NIGHT SPOT, ARGENTINA

It's '92. And there's an eclipse coming up this year. And it's in dear old South America, Thelma's and my third go at the continent. The total solar eclipse will be a little different. It will be at sunrise in Uruguay! Thelma and I will be there.

We signed up with a California group specializing in eclipse trips. It was operated - I guess he was the boss - by a chubby little guy named Ernie Moser. As far as I'm concerned, he could not have done a better job of arranging our itinerary. We flew to Rio de Janeiro as we did in '75. We met the rest of our group in our hotel on Copacabana Beach before touring the city.

The one attraction nobody misses in Rio is the giant statue of Jesus Christ entitled "Christ the Redeemer". We had to take a small train to get up the high peak upon which it stood. There is not all that much room up there on the top, but one had to stand back some to get the full effect of the icon. So, they built a lengthy observation masonry platform in one direction - westerly, I believe. The statue was impressive when viewed from the end of the walkway. Then we rode the Sugar Loaf aerial car - an exhilarating ride and an equally exhilarating mountaintop view of Rio and its ocean-caressing location. Sensational!

The next day we swam from Copacabana Beach. Smooth sand, gentle waves and occasionally a tall and slender topless beauty would glide on by. But she looked straight ahead, not at me. (Really the 'Girl from Ipanema', but it applies here). The wives in the group weren't all that impressed. Anyway, it was a refreshing swim in the Atlantic.

Our itinerary called for a flight to where Brazil, Argentina and Paraguay meet - Iquasu Falls. Niagara Falls is higher, but that's the only superlative it has over Iguasu Falls - the area of water tumbling over land is vast. At one point, we went to one of the cataracts into which they had built a stone or concrete platform. One could go down to the lower level of the falls and watch the water tumbling down in front of you. You didn't get soaked, but you got sprayed pretty good. At the time we were there (June), there had been much rain upstream. This caused the water to be tannish/red in color carrying soil runoff as it did.

We stayed at a small but fine hotel nearby with toucans, parrots and cockatoos flying around on the grounds and coati, raccoon-like creatures, looking for handouts.

Our next flight took us to Montevideo, Uruguay. Like Buenos Aires which we had seen in '75, Montevideo reminded one of Paris in its architecture. We had to bus to Punta del Este some 50/60 miles east to be in position for the sunrise eclipse, a first for Thelma and me.

We were roused at 5 AM to pile into the bus to travel 20 or so miles more to the east. We wound up at a private beach club (Club de Mars). Since this was winter in the southern hemisphere, the place was seemingly deserted. But we roused the caretaker personnel.

We were on the beach looking to the east and where we expected the eclipsed sun to rise. It did, although there were many clouds around. The partially eclipsed sun came up as a golden spike sticking straight up out of the sea. And it left a golden reflection on the surface of the Atlantic. I tell you it was awesome, at the risk of being repetitive. But just about as soon as it was due to morph into totality, the low-lying clouds took over. When tallying up my roster of total solar eclipses seen, I don't count this one. Others in the group will say they saw it, but I don't believe them. That is not to say that it wasn't a spectacular event - it was, but no TSE.

The last stop on our great South American tour was Buenos Aires, Argentina. It was interesting to see, like Thelma's and my home in DC, that they had an obelisk monument similar to the Washington Monument. We toured the city by bus, went to "The City of the Dead" - a cemetery filled with beautiful memorials, monuments and vaults. Two memorial vaults which we saw in particular were the one for Eva Perón and another for Luis Firpo, a former world's heavyweight boxing champion. A pampas cattle ranch, an estancia, was also on the agenda with food and music.

But the lasting memory Thelma and I will have of this city was an evening trip to a nightclub where couples exhibited the tango. It's strange. When we traveled South America and Buenos Aires seventeen years earlier, Thelma wanted to see a tango show. It didn't appeal to me then and we didn't go. I regretted so much that decision after that. But here in '92, we had a chance to correct that mistake - one doesn't often get a second chance to make things right. The show was great and the music, especially the accordion player, was superb.

But once again it was time to head back north and home. But we added many an appealing memory to those tapes in our brains.

Sugar Loaf Aerial Ride, Rio de Janeiro, Brazil

Rio Beach Scene

ARRANGED FOR THELMA MARTIN'S FUNERAL & AFFAIRS AFTER HER SUDDEN DEATH BY HEART ATTACK - 1993

STAYED IN APARTMENT OVERLOOKING GOVERNORS ISLAND & LOWER MANHATTAN

Up in my apartment on the fourth floor, I received a call from Thelma's cleaning lady. She was working in Thelma's apartment when Thelma fell to the floor. She called 911 and me. I went down to her apartment immediately and the Emergency Medical people arrived soon after. They worked on her for some time and then decided to take her to George Washington Hospital. I rode with them in the front of the ambulance.

Once during the trip to the hospital they stopped the ambulance, I presume to administer more life-saving procedures. Later, I waited in the hospital waiting room for perhaps twenty minutes. I was called in to the emergency room where they told me she was gone. I saw her there on the gurney in the hospital. My lifelong companion of 42 years was still. One hospital lady told me not to hesitate to call her if she could be of any assistance at all. I don't believe I ever did.

Debra Newman, who Thelma liked to call her "play daughter", was very helpful in making the necessary arrangements. Since Thelma loved New York so much, we decided to have the funeral there in her Bronx neighborhood. When Thelma converted to Catholicism later in life, she was counseled by one Father Manning. He traveled from Washington and made arrangements with the Bronx church to have the funeral ceremony. Father Manning and Debra both provided a moving eulogy and homily.

Needless to say, I missed that lady very much. She had been with me on so many trips to various parts of the world (except the USSR). She was a trooper! We had seen six total solar eclipses together. We two New Yorkers had so much in common, but nothing, I suppose, is everlasting. Maybe we'll be together again - who knows.

I was invited to stay overnight in Debbie's apartment. The Brooklyn place was maybe eight stories high overlooking downtown Manhattan, the Manhattan ferry slip of the Staten Island ferry and Governors Island. The apartment had a spectacular view encompassing as it did the confluence of the East and Hudson Rivers. One could stare for an hour watching the boats traveling constantly up and down the harbor. Quite a sight.

RAN 5K & 10K ROAD RACES, US SENIOR OLYMPICS, BATON ROUGE, LA. – 1993

Just about a month after Thelma's death, I was scheduled to run in the five kilometer and ten kilometer road races in Louisiana. When I participated successfully in the DC Senior Games before her death, I became eligible to participate in the US Senior Olympics in Baton Rouge. Most events were held on the campus of Louisiana State University. I was conflicted as to whether or not I should go, but I finally came down on the side of going.

I didn't win any medals in either race, but as the losers usually say, the joy is in the competing. Of course, this was a great opportunity to visit New Orleans, a first for me. Also on the agenda was a New Orleans harbor cruise on a stern wheel river boat, the 'Natchez'. Later, I checked out the Latin Quarter and Bourbon Street. Food sampling was not ignored.

It's a shame I could not have made the trip more successful by winning a medal or two, but the competition, being country-wide, was too tough for me. Well, maybe next time. There was one other noteworthy event for the week - my cousin Louise Murphy Mongi from Pennsylvania, five years older than me, entered one of the swimming events and did well in her age group. She was a member of the Women's Swimming Association as a young adult. I think it was good for me to get away from Washington if only for a week. The trip was a healthy diversion.

Fellow Senior Olympians, Bator Rouge, Louisiana

FLEW IN 4-SEATER AIRCRAFT FROM RYE, NY TO GEORGE WASHINGTON BRIDGE, NY/NJ AND BACK - 1993

After Thelma's death, Carole DiFrancesca and Brian Calen whom we met on the eclipse trip to Brazil/Argentina/Uruguay, invited me to stay with them for awhile in their house in Dobbs Ferry, New York. I combined the trip with one to see my cousin Irene and her husband George in Newburgh, NY. It was very nice of the Calen's to invite me to their home for an overnight stay.

Brian is young and very adventurous. He found a way to entertain me, although it wasn't necessary, with an non-ordinary event. He and his girlfriend (they were married within a year or so) and I would rent a four-seater aircraft out of nearby Rye, NY and fly around for an hour or so. Hey, I was game if they were.

At a small terminal building we waited for awhile before climbing aboard the plane. The pilot and Brian were up front and Carole and I occupied the rear seats. With a real loud noise, we took off, not too smoothly, into the wind.

At first we flew over either Brian's or Carole's folks place. They had told them they would be flying over at a particular time, so they waved as did we. I'm not sure I saw them on the ground, but Brian says he did. They asked me if I wanted to fly someplace and I told them I would like to see upper Manhattan (my original neighborhood) and the George Washington Bridge over the Hudson connecting New York with New Jersey. And we did. I had my trusty camera and took pictures of Inwood in Manhattan and treasure the best one to this day. Carole seemed uncharacteristically quiet during the flight and I got the impression, maybe erroneously, that she wished we were back on terra firma. I guess I wouldn't have minded that prospect either. But all too soon we headed back to Rye and had a smooth landing. That's another great experience - thanks again, Brian.

I'm so thankful Brian came up with this suggestion. It was a wonderful diversion from all that had happened these last several months. Soon I had to get back to Washington, but not before Brian and I made plans for seeing an annular (ring) eclipse due in upstate New York the following year.

With the Calen's – Carole & Brian

STAYED IN APARTMENT WITH EMPIRE STATE B. TO WEST AND CHRYSLER B. TO NORTH - 1993

There came a time when I had to go to New York to check on Thelma Martin's Bronx house which she bequeathed to me. At about this time, I was also in touch with my second cousin Lori, my cousin Irene's daughter. She had married a Brazilian musician, he played the double bass mostly, and they had set up housekeeping in an apartment in midtown New York City. They both worked in the area, so it was quite convenient for them. I'm not sure, but I think they were living there on a temporary basis until the owner returned from someplace. Lori invited me to crash at her place for a night where I met Rogério.

As to the apartment, it was on about the tenth floor and it was on Park Avenue at 34th or 35th Streets. Lori had both western and northern exposures, although the apartment wasn't very large. But it did have these beautiful views. To the west was the one-time record holder in building height - the Empire State Building - standing there so tall and erect and looking like royalty in architecture. And if you walked around a corner of the apartment into the small kitchen you could see out the north-facing window the slim and shining Chrysler Building, also a former record holder until eclipsed by none other than the Empire State Building. Both buildings were less than a half mile distant from our vantage point at the windows.

That evening I suggested to Lori about going up to the top of the Empire State Building to which she readily agreed. So up we went just like in a Hollywood movie. The air was clear and the scene was magical as twilight turned to darkness - another memory not soon forgotten. Lori took the opportunity to inquire about her grandmother, my aunt. As aunts and nephews go, we were quite close, so I think I may have given her some new perspectives about her maternal grandmother. I was happy to tell her all I knew.

With Cousin Lori's Husband's Bull Fiddle

AWED BY PERFECT ANNULAR (RING) ECLIPSE NEAR UTICA, NY - 1994

In my first visit to Brian's place in Dobbs Ferry, NY, we had read about an annular (ring) eclipse passing through upper New York state on Tuesday, May 3, 1994. Of course, Brian was very interested in "bagging" this one, as was I. Neither of us had ever seen an annular (although Thelma and I had tried in Virginia in '84), so we set up plans to go for it.

The track would go through northern Ohio, northwestern Pennsylvania, south of Rochester, NY and just north of Syracuse and Utica, NY. The center line would continue through the Adirondacks, Vermont and New Hampshire. Brian and I decided, in advance by phone, that I would come up to stay in his house and then we would go in his car to a motel in the Syracuse area. Carole couldn't go because of commitments, but Brian's uncle came.

On the big day, the sky looked not too promising for an eclipse. To be sure, the sun was shining, but sporadically. Clouds dominated. Of course, we checked the TV weather people who gave us some mixed signals. They said the clouds were coming in off Lake Ontario and would likely dissipate by late morning - about the time of the eclipse. Also, they indicated there was probably less of an overcast further inland from the lake. I halfheartedly opted to remain in the Syracuse area until eclipse time, but Brian thought we should travel further east - perhaps the Utica area - which I did not object to.

Subsequently, we did head east to Utica, then north towards the center line. Clouds were still present as we got a bite to eat somewhere near our proposed viewing area. We found an open field off the road where we parked the car and Brian set up his equipment. By now the sky was clearing rapidly. By eclipse time, miraculously, the sky in the sun's direction was cloudless. Brian's decision was vindicated completely. Thanks again Brian!

Although I did not bring my trusty thermometer, pictures taken before the event show us with jackets on but no gloves - the temperature must have been in the upper 40's or 50's. They also show clouds in the background and a weak sun shining, so the timing of the cloud clearing was exquisite.

And the actual annular eclipse was an awesome sight, to use that word again. After the partial phase, a thin, perfect ring of bright yellow sunshine, surrounding a black orb, in a darkened blue sky presented itself. Wow! What an out of this world vista. We'll never forget it.

Getting back to Dobbs Ferry required traveling east along the Mohawk trail, in some places along a restored Erie Canal (opened in 1825). I call this eclipse "The Mohawk Ring".

PLIED WATERS OF LAKE TITICACA, BOLIVIAN/ PERUVIAN BORDER - 1994

WITNESSED NEAR TOTAL SOLAR ECLIPSE ON STREETS OF LA PAZ, BOL.

We had a fine opportunity to talk, Brian Calen and I, about plans for the next total solar eclipse. But distance made one think. It would pass through central South America including southern Bolivia. There was another great but expensive trip to northern Chile. Brian and I were desirous of a more cost-effective trip (read cheaper).

Brian hopped on the phone when we got back to his place. As only Brian can, he dug up some deal where we would fly to La Paz, Bolivia on our own and at a pretty good price. We would go with another eclipse chasing buddy from the Uruguayan junket by name Peter Williams from Vancouver, BC, Canada. We had planned to rent a jeep and travel south of the city on the altiplano and set up a tent (we had our sleeping bags) to be on site early on the morning of Thursday, November 3, 1994.

We were in La Paz several days early, had rented the jeep and tooled around La Paz to get a feel for the driving and roads. The high plain has an elevation of about 12,000 feet, enough to make you suck wind under moderate exertion. We also took a trip down to Lake Titicaca, the highest lake in the world on which steamboats ply. We were there on a beautiful morning and took a launch across the southern part of the lake to an island.

On these jeep trips, I was usually consigned to the back of the jeep. There was a lot of jostling in the back on uncomfortable, side-facing seats. I don't know whether it was the thought of being bounced around for 200 miles in the back of a jeep or if it was the dreaded siroche (altitude sickness), but on the big day I was sick. I felt bad. The prospect of the ride and the headache made me decide to skip the trip south to see the total solar eclipse. Very likely one of my worst decisions ever.

So Brian and Peter left early while I was sleeping in. I eventually got up and saw the 95% partial eclipse in La Paz. There were quite a few other people (La Pazians?) staring through their sun filters at the partial phase on the streets during the morning hours. It was all very intriguing.

The boys returned and, according to their reports, were very successful. They saw it all in clear skies. Of course, as the years go by, I could question my sanity for traveling some 8000 miles round trip and chickening out at almost the last minute, but I was 71 years of age and feeling very poorly at the time and at the prospect of the journey and I made my decision. Except for the missed total solar eclipse opportunity, it was a great trip to La Paz, Bolivia, Lake Titicaca and the altiplano, one which will be remembered for the rest of my life, even though it could have been much better (or possibly much worse).

On the Altiplano, Bolivia

PLED SUCCESSFULLY BEFORE DC JUDGE FOR EVICTION OF NON-PAYING TENANT - 1996

Maybe six to twelve months after Thelma Martin's death, I moved from my fourth floor apartment into her larger apartment on the first floor of our condominium building. I was kept busy in those days conducting apartment sales of unwanted and excess furniture, household goods and appliances.

Also, of course, I was in contact with Thelma's relatives, or at least one in particular, living in North Carolina. One of Thelma's first cousins was named Hettie Lucinda Burnett Wingfield. She was a longtime widow. We corresponded by telephone and mail and eventually traded visits.

But I digress. After moving into the first floor apartment, I decided to rent out the fourth floor efficiency apartment I had previously called my home for about 30 years. Now my life was largely occupied by talking to real estate people and composing and placing ads on local bulletin boards and in the local newspaper. Finally, one gentleman rented the apartment and was a good tenant for perhaps six months before falling behind with his rent payments.

After missing several promised deadlines to pay me my due, I instigated action at the DC Courthouse - a matter of getting the correct forms, filling them out and submitting them to the proper authorities. It is nice to have the law backing you up. A court date was established and I appeared before the judge. When he heard the circumstances of the case, he ruled in my favor.

Getting a favorable ruling and getting the money owed me, however, are two separate things. He jumped town. The tracer organization I hired to find his whereabouts could not locate him. Eventually I had to swallow my loss, but, I suppose, I learned a lesson. The lesson was to be more careful when dealing with valuables. But in my case, the lesson was to not be a landlord! After one more attempt at renting, I finally sold the condominium apartment which worked out much better for me.

WON PRIZES FOR WINNING CONTEST ON NAMING CONDO NEWSLETTER, DC – 1997

One day early in the year a contest was run to determine a new name for the newsletter of the condominium I was living in. The existing name was awkward because the name of the condo itself was awkward. It was called Carrollsburg Square originally.

Now, the 'Carroll' part of the condo name is of historical significance. In the days preceding the birth of the United States of America, one of the important landowners in the area was Charles Carroll of Carrollton, Maryland. Before the District of Columbia was formed, the land belong to the state of Maryland. A section of the now southwest quadrant of the new city was named after Charles Carroll and called Carrollsburg. To choose to name a condo in the area 'Carrollsburg Square' was natural and significant.

But the condo title was long and awkward, particularly in subsequent days of short, terse titles. My thinking was that the title of the monthly newsletter should retain some of the old name, but in a shorter, punchier version. Thus, I decided on 'C'burg'. And to go with C'burg, of course, I chose the alliterative 'Scene'. "C'burg Scene" was my entry for the newsletter's title. Apparently, it clicked with the judges: the name was chosen.

I received five or six gift certificates, and promises of free items, from various shops in the mall across the street as my prize. I enjoyed the modest fame the contest winner accrued and the small bounty of goods and services that resulted there from. No longer, however, could I claim that I've never won anything in my life (although it wasn't a million dollars)!

TOOK FUTURE WIFE ON HER FIRST FLIGHT TO SEE MY BROTHER BILL IN NAPLES, FL. - 1997

After Thelma Martin died, I got in touch with her relatives in eastern North Carolina. When Thelma and I were together, she hardly mentioned her relatives. She always talked about her life in New York City, her schooling in Berkeley, California, and her employment in Washington, DC. Was she somewhat ashamed of her mother's "country folk"? Maybe so, but I subsequently learned that she visited with them at least once, though I don't remember her having done so, but her cousin had pictures to prove it.

But as mentioned previously, I got in contact with her first cousin - Hettie Lucinda Burnett Wingfield. We corresponded by mail and talked, more and more frequently, on the phone. We seemed to hit it off. She was a widow, her husband Craig Wingfield, a WW II veteran having died many years earlier. I got to calling her Lu.

We met for the first time about a year after Thelma's death when she visited some friends in Maryland. Like Thelma, she was seven years older than me, but people were genuinely amazed when they found out her age; she seemed so much younger. We courted for three years or so, both in DC and in Hubert near Jacksonville, NC, making side trips in the areas and taking walks in both locales. I know I was smitten and I'm sure she was too.

I eventually popped the question in the car after picking her up one rainy January night. She said yes and made me a happy man. We set the date for June. We had three problems, however. We were both full-fledged senior citizens, she just turned 80 and I, my mid-seventies. Secondly, she lived in North Carolina and I in DC - a matter of 350 miles or so. And finally, she was African-American and I, European-American. Neither of us cared at all about these things, but I wondered how my Florida-living brother, sister-in-law and three kids would take it. All were born and raised in New York and, except for my niece Linda, moved to Florida fifteen or so years earlier.

So, we managed to get an invitation to come down to see them for three or four days in May. All went smoothly. Lu took it like a trooper for what must have been a difficult trip for her. We flew round-trip and it was her first aircraft flights. She excepted that experience without a whimper. I think I've got me a fine one here. This old bachelor is getting married in a month!

MARRIED AT 74 TO 80 YEAR YOUNG BLACK LADY, HETTIE LU BURNETT, DC - 1997

WRITTEN UP, OUR MARRIAGE, IN WASHINGTON POST FEATURE ARTICLE

June 21, 1997 - the longest day of the year - finally rolled around on the calendar. A really nice neighbor, Jim Rule, offered to manage our wedding. It would be held in the grassy central plaza of our three-high-rise, townhouse condominium complex in Southwest, DC. Jim took a liking to us, kidding us every time he saw us walking in the area. He and his housemate were gay, but it didn't matter in the least to us.

We had an unexpectedly large number of people attend our outdoor wedding on a very warm day. Lu's niece, a federal employee in the higher echelons of the Department of Homeland Security, fulfilled the role of Maid of Honor. My brother Bill, after having driven up from Florida with his wife Jean, was my Best Man and returned the favor when I was his Best Man 43 years earlier! Lu's foster brother, McKinley Hunter, gave the bride away.

With Jim Rule's direction and the numerous volunteers who assisted him, all went smoothly; although Lu later told me that she almost fainted with the heat and excitement. There was quite an audience between Lu's relatives and friends from North Carolina, Massachusetts, Chicago and New York. Lu had cared for a pair of infant twins in her younger days in NY and they came down from the north as married women to witness her ceremony. Many others in the group were Carrollsburg neighbors. Ours was the first wedding ever held at the complex (and maybe the last!).

The 'Young' Bride & Groom, Washington, DC

Carrollsburg Condominium Meeting Room

INVITED BY GUARD, WIFE AND I, TO JOIN PUBLIC TOUR OF WHITE HOUSE - 1997

A few weeks after Lu and I were married, we were walking near the White House as I was showing her around town. We did a lot of car riding and walking during our courtship. One day I sat down and listed the places around the capital area we had been to, and came up with this list. We both were amazed at the length of the list. In no particular order:

Lady Bird Johnson Park across the Potomac on the Virginia shore

Visit to Potomac Mills, a large mall in Virginia

Inspected US Capitol Christmas Tree on the Capitol lawn

Viewed National Arboretum azaleas in NE, Washington

Tidal Basin Cherry Blossoms, the world famous ring of flowers

Trip to Great Falls, Maryland, to see the falls & C & O Canal

National Zoo in Rock Creek Park, including the giant pandas

"Spirit of Washington" Potomac cruise down to Mt. Vernon, VA

Tour of George Washington's Mount Vernon home

Car trip visit to Damascus Md. to visit some of Lu's friends

Lunch and movies at DC's newly refurbished Union Station

The Hains Point "Giant" sculpture - The Awakening

Dined at Jenny's Chinese restaurant in SW, DC

Walked around restored Glen Echo Amusement Park

Gazed at National Christmas Tree on ellipse near White House

Fed ducks and squirrels on DC waterfront walks

Trip to New York, overnight stay at Ramada Inn, the Bronx

Visited Ford's Theater and House Where Lincoln Died

Smithsonian Air & Space Museum for I-Max movie and lunch

Saw "King Mackerel" and Christmas concert at Kennedy Center

National Cemetery Tomb of Unknown Soldier & JFK Memorial

And last but not least, the White House inspection. We were standing around near the front of the long line of people waiting to see the President's House. I don't know if the guard recognized us from the Post article or if he took pity on the two senior citizens, but he personally invited us to go into the historical building. We didn't hesitate.

Although I had been in Washington, DC for 47 years, I had never visited the famed building, occupied by every US president save one - George Washington. As a native New Yorker, I had never been to the Statue of Liberty until Thelma and I went in 1986.

As to the White House, the rooms seemed large and airy to us. The rooms, with their special names, were well lit and bright. It would be a nice place to live if only there weren't so many people traipsing in and out of the place!

SOLD NY HOUSE & DC CONDO AND RENTED OUT ANOTHER ONE - 1997

BOUGHT AND MOVED TO HOUSE IN NEW BERN, NC

As mentioned, Thelma Martin, bless her heart, left her NY Bronx house to me in her will. Although born in Manhattan, she grew up in the Bronx and loved both areas. The area in the Bronx where the house was situated was an enclave of private family homes and small family-run shops. I enjoyed going to her neighborhood very much.

But, the house didn't fit into my plans for the future. I took steps, first, to update the windows, doors and insulation and second, to have a realtor, and eventually a lawyer, arrange for the sale of the house. It took some months and entailed some complications, but in a few months it was accomplished to my complete satisfaction. So much for the out-of-state house sale.

As to our condo apartments in DC, I moved into Thelma's one bedroom place and out of my efficiency apartment. After making several less than successful attempts at renting the fourth floor efficiency, I decided to put it up for sale. Once again the sale was accomplished rather quickly and to my satisfaction. So much for one of the condos.

Lu and I were married in June of '97. We lived in the first floor apartment, but decided to move to North Carolina. I thought it would be closer to my brother and sister-in-law in Florida (but not too close) and closer to Lu's relatives in Jacksonville, NC (but not too close). We decided on New Bern - an historical town close (but not too close) to the Atlantic beaches.

I obtained literature from New Bern after having read an article about the town. Soon after, we engaged the services of a realtor who showed us what was available in the town's housing market. We also investigated the Jacksonville, NC area, but preferred the more historical and less military-oriented New Bern area. Jacksonville is home to Camp Lejeune and the Marine Corps.

We got help for our long distance move (for a price). So, we eventually sold the one bedroom condo apartment and moved lock, stock and cat (Sandy) to a purchased house in a suburb of New Bern called River Bend in October.

Lu and I were so happy there for nine years, but life has a way of interfering. There will be more on this aspect later. And so much for all the houses and condos. What a year! We were glad it was over.

WALKED/JOGGED 15,072 MILES IN 32.5 YEARS, EAST POTOMAC PARK, DC - 1997

Golf is quite popular in Washington, DC and its surroundings. DC must have three or four public 18 hole courses, not to mention the Maryland and Virginia links. So it was natural that I would take up this sport for its exercise and entertainment value.

My fellow employees and I would meet mostly every Sunday morning at the courses (in the later years at the West Potomac Park public course). We would have to place our golf bags on the "wheel", a devise assuring a first-come-first-served policy. The catch is, if you don't do this by, say, 6 AM, you would have to spend a lot of time waiting to play and waist a good part of your Sunday day off.

After about 8 or 10 years of this, it dawned on me one day; I'm having fun, yes, but rising at 5:30 AM on Sunday morning itself is not much fun and the exercise I was getting was limited to sporadic walking. I started walking off the course and later around the perimeter of the course, or Hains Point as is its name. I settled on a six mile or 10 kilometer length on Sunday morning. This began on January 17, 1965. I can remember so specifically because I kept a written record of my times and the weather conditions. For example, on that January day, which happened to be my father's 79th birthday, the temperature was 13 degrees, the wind was from the north at 17 MPH, the sky was cloudless, the visibility or air density was unlimited and, of course, there was no precipitation. There was some snow on the ground. I didn't start keeping track of my times for the six miles until September of that year when I did the six in 104 minutes.

I maintained the habit, with a few variations here and there, for 32 and a half years until we moved to North Carolina after our wedding. My best time, or personal record (or PR, as they say) for the six miles was 49 minutes flat on December 4, 1977.

The 15,072 miles designated in the above leader includes a good estimate of other than Sunday walks around the park and the town. Walking was my hobby I guess you could say.

CRUISED CARIBBEAN SEA ON 50,000 TON MS RYNDAM - 1998

SAW DOMINICA FROM GUADELOUPE, 50 MILES DISTANT

We delayed our honeymoon trip for eight months to coincide with - what else - a total solar eclipse in the Caribbean due on February 26, 1998. This would be Lu's first and my seventh TSE if we had a successful sighting.

We utilized the tour services of an old friend, Virginia Roth out of Florida. She specialized in eclipse trips. She had us sailing on the Holland America Line's MS Ryndam. This TSE would be primarily over water - the Pacific, the Caribbean and the Atlantic, hence, the boat trip.

We had many of our old eclipse buddies with us including Carole and Brian Calen. It was a fun trip as we stopped at Guadeloupe, St. Martin/Maarten, St. Thomas, Barbados and the Line's own Half Moon Cay in the Bahamas. We had a great stateroom for our honeymoon trip as it was located central to most of the important shipboard activities.

We toured Guadeloupe on a bus. Among other places, we stopped to view Crawfish Falls. But an episode that impressed me took place on the way there. At one point, the bus stopped and the tour guide pointed out on the horizon the neighboring island of Dominica. The air was so clear we could see it even though it was fifty miles away. Even the seasoned guide was surprised.

As to the eclipse, it went off like clockwork on a beautiful Caribbean morning. We assembled our group primarily on the forward open deck below and in front of the bridge. Our tour leader/ astronomer Richard T. Feinberg kept us informed of important timing events over the ship's loud speaker system. My wife Lu was enthralled by her first total solar eclipse. As usual, I kept track of the temperatures before, during and after the event. This was the warmest eclipse of my seven eclipses with the temperatures 94, 84 and 87 (F), respectively. Come to think of it, it was probably my warmest February 26th, period.

We enjoyed everything about the trip, although at one point, I was starting to bump into my life's ceiling. When trying out for snorkeling, I just about tired myself out just donning the equipment! I did get to see some colorful fish beneath the water's surface, but I decided to head back to shore to get some rest. Three years later, the medics had me undergo a triple bypass coronary surgery. I'm sure now that I wasn't the guy I used to be.

But all too soon, we were back in Ft. Lauderdale, Fl., saying our goodbyes and heading to the airport. We loved the ship which was our home for a week, the MS Ryndam.

Set for Caribbean Total Solar Eclipse

Lu Burnett Ward, Honeymoon Trip, (RYNDAM in rear)

With Guide Monique & Driver Pietro, Munich, Germany

ENJOYED ICE CREAM ON SHORE OF DANUBE RIVER NEAR LINZ, AUSTRIA - 1999

RODE GIANT FERRIS WHEEL, PRATER AMUSEMENT PARK, VIENNA

There was going to be a humdinger of a total solar eclipse this year. I decided to pull a fast one and not go with a group, but instead, my wife Lu and I would travel on our own to Europe. Lu hadn't been there and I hadn't been there since 1992 to see ballerina Virginia Johnson. But where in Europe?

But a little about the eclipse. Why was it so special? First of all, it would be the last TSE of the 20th Century - what a way to finish "my" century. I say "my" century since I lived for more than 75 years in it. Secondly, it would occur in the benign month of August. Thirdly, it would cross Europe diagonally from England to Bulgaria and Turkey and finish in India. This one eclipse would probably be seen by more people than any other in history considering its path and the burgeoning world population.

Lu and I visited our travel agent and she tried to accommodate our desires - a cheaper trip to Europe which would stop to look at an eclipse. We decided on Austria as the eclipse would pass from near Salzburg and exit Austria to the east of Vienna. Our group trip in Austria would visit both cities.

In the inevitable introductions of tour members, several of us indicated that we hoped the tour would take the time to witness the heavenly event. Since it wasn't on the schedule, it would have to be a chancy proposition. But from what I could tell, all of Europe was fairly excited about the event. On the big day, we were traveling by bus from Salzburg to Vienna. All along the highway people were stopping their cars on the shoulder and gazing up at the sun through special eclipse glasses.

Our group was directed by a pretty Dutch girl (Monique) and our bus was driven by an Italian (Pietro). They did stop along the highway at the proper time for all of us to pile out and catch the last TSE of the 1900's. Beautiful timing. I was so happy I teared up.

Our group missed out on a short cruise down the Danube because of our unscheduled stop. Too bad. But we had a leisurely wait at our riverfront destination. Lu and I sat at a table and casually ate ice cream while watching boats glide up and down the beautiful blue Danube (which was tan at the time) - as if we did this every day!

On to Vienna. We find it difficult to believe we're here. The ferris wheel, with room-sized passenger compartments and featured in the old movie "The Third Man", was an interesting and unusual added episode for us in the magnificent city. These people are so clean judging by their immaculate capital city.

HAVE SEEN, WITH ONE IN AUSTRIA, EIGHT TOTAL SOLAR ECLIPSES IN MY LIFETIME - 1999

Perhaps a summary would be in order here concerning total solar eclipses I have witnessed:

1. 1970 - Sandbridge Virginia with Thelma Martin
2. 1979 - Roundup, Montana with Thelma
3. 1980 - Ancola, India with Thelma
4. 1981 - Bratsk, USSR alone in group
5. 1988 - Celebes Sea off Indonesia with Thelma
6. 1991 - Baja California, Mexico with Thelma
7. 1998 - Caribbean Sea off Guadeloupe, Leewards with Lu Ward
8. 1999 - On the road, Salzburg to Linz, Austria with Lu

These eight were the "gold standard" of eclipse watching - total solar eclipses. The above list does not include beautiful partial events and the near misses, such as happened to me in Mattice, Ontario, Canada in 1954, Punta del Este, Uruguay, 1992 and La Paz, Bolivia, 1994. Also not included is the perfect annular (ring) eclipse of 1994 near Utica, New York, one of the prettiest sights of them all.

Some of the VIPs we met on these trips included:

1. Astronaut Scott Carpenter
2. Meteorologist Dr. Edward M. Brooks
3. Astronaut Michael Collins
4. Astronomer Dr. Bart Bok
5. TV astronomer Jack Horkheimer
6. Actor Tony Curtis
7. Astronomer Richard Feinberg
8. Magazine editor, Sky & Telescope, Leif J. Robinson

I like to think that I'm still pursuing the darn things as I write this. But age, finances, travel difficulties all conspire to limit the activity. There will be a knockout TSE crossing our own country (USA) in August, 2017 and passing within 150 miles of my current home. My dream is to keep in some kind of shape for that one. But, I'd be 94 years of age - possibly I might catch it, but, unfortunately quite unlikely. Still, one has to have a dream, a plan, a purpose in life to look forward to. Well, I've got one.

Baja California, Mexico – Total Solar Eclipse

WATCHED DOLPHINS PLAY IN OUR BOAT WAKE, EVERGLADES, FL. - 2000

This year, my wife Lu and I rode the cement and asphalt strip known as I-95, down to Florida to see my brother Bill and his wife Jean. It's a long haul by car from eastern North Carolina to southern Florida, but if you break it up into two segments, it's not so bad. We saw their new beautiful house near Naples and they took us out to lunch and dinner. We saw Naples up close and a lovely town it is, and one day we all went to a Native/American-run casino nearby.

One morning, however, we took off on our own for the southernmost part of Everglades Park. We boarded a boat which would ply the inland and coastal mangrove waters of the park. It was a wonderful day and the cruise was exceedingly educational and fun-filled.

I suppose the highlight of the trip was being overtaken in our boat by a pod (if that's the word) of dolphins. They approached us out of nowhere from the rear and played along in our wake for maybe five minutes. They would at times leap clear of the water in a horizontal attitude, so that you could see their entire sleek and shining bodies not more than 20 feet or so from our eyes. It was a wondrous sight to behold. It's also a wonder no one fell over the railings in the excitement - but they didn't.

All too soon we had to head back to the north country, but we did so with a double overnight stop in Orlando where we took in EPCOT. All in all, Lu and I had a great vacation. Everything went according to plan and the enjoyment was full and complete.

By Launch through the Everglades, Florida

WON CAMERA IN PUTTING CONTEST ON SECOND TRIP ON MS RYNDAM - 2000

RODE PASSED SOUTHERNMOST POINT OF CONTINENTAL USA, KEY WEST, FL

Lu and I liked our honeymoon cruise on the MS Ryndam in '98 so much, we decided to do it again on the same ship. We specified that we wanted to get our old stateroom back; they could not accede to our desire, but said a mirror-image of the room was open on the other side of the ship. We naturally took it.

We felt more at ease and comfortable on this trip, since we didn't have to "get to know" the ship as we did on the '98 eclipse trip.

Then we met our dinner companions. They were a middle-aged couple from California. We found it easier to warm up to him before we got to know his wife. They were the Scotts, John and Elinor of El Toro. We weren't sure in the beginning if the four of us would be compatible, but after five meals we were "Christmas Card-exchanging buddies".

One day I decided to enter the ship's putting contest. As indicated previously, I had played golf years before, but hadn't indulged much since then. But, what the heck! We putted on a carpeted open spot, not far from our stateroom actually. The ship's people had set up hoops, sort of like croquet hoops, through which we had to putt the golf ball. After nine 'holes', I think, me and another guy were tied with the same number of strokes. The rules called for a run-off at the end of which we were tied again! Finally, a one-hole sudden death play-off allowed me to walk off with the prize - a pre-loaded, take-to-the-drugstore camera. It was a lot of fun.

One of our stops was Key West, Fl. We took the "train" tour, one of those motorized engine and train deals that ply the city's streets. It's a remarkable town. So sunny (when we were there) and green and flowered. Ernest Hemmingway's House was pointed out (I saw no cats). Our tour was interrupted for 15 minutes or so as a car and bicycle accident occurred just in front of us on a narrow street. Our "train" couldn't back up to bypass the accident. Hopefully, no significant injury occurred.

Finally, we stopped at the southernmost point in the continental USA. The spot is marked by a colorfully painted, pointy, barrel-like structure. Just think, everybody in the continental US, without exception, was to the north of us at that very moment! I like that kind of unusual stuff.

UNDERWENT SUCCESSFULLY, TRIPLE BYPASS CORONARY SURGERY, NC - 2001

One day I went to my doctor for what I expected would be a routine checkup. I think I told him that I seemed to get tired more than I did usually. I didn't think it was such a big deal.

But, I suppose, that set the wheels in motion. Dr. Lather had me see a heart specialist, then the specialist had me, with my permission of course, go out of town to undergo an angiogram. As a side note, this was done on September 11, 2001, the infamous day when terrorist's hijacked planes brought down New York's Twin Towers. I was just regaining consciousness when the mayhem started. Of course, we viewed it on television.

The angiogram apparently convinced the doctors that I required bypass surgery and they convinced me that I needed the operation. I felt good otherwise, so it was a surprise to me that this was necessary. But, so be it. A date was set which had to be delayed when I seemed to have a cold. Finally, early October proved to be the time to go under the knife.

Apparently, the operation was successful and went off without a hitch. I was surprised again when they told me later that it was a triple bypass operation.

It took several months before I could get back to my old routine. But everything, seven years later, seems to be working properly as far as I can detect. I still get my daily walks completed and my Sunday "long" walk (1 hour/3.5 miles) completed and in the books.

Guess I'm a fortunate man.

SPENT WEEK ON DOCKED RMS QUEEN MARY, LONG BEACH, CAL. - 2002

TOLD QUEEN MARY TOUR GROUP OF 1943 WARTIME TRIP AND GOT HAND

TOOK LAUNCH TO SANTA CATALINA ISLAND FROM LONG BEACH, CAL.

It's been a goal of mine to revisit some of my old WW II locales. Most are in Europe, of course, but not all. Many old places are no longer in existence or at least not as they were 60 odd years ago. But one was sitting at a dock outside Long Beach, California - the RMS Queen Mary.

As described previously, I went to Europe as a soldier in 1943. We were on the ship for eight/ nine days, although the passage itself was only five days plus seven hours. We had plenty of time to roam that ship in '43, me and my buddies.

I noticed there was an Elderhostel trip to Long Beach that would utilize the big ship as a hotel, but when I inquired, it turned out it didn't suit our timetable. So we, wife Lu and I, decided to do it on our own. We flew to Los Angeles (LAX) and, not seeing any public transportation to Long Beach, decided to take a cab. It got us to the Mary all right - for $40.

We checked in at the front desk and finally got our stateroom. It was a long day - we were happy to stop the rushing around and start the relaxing.

Our stateroom was one level below the Promenade Deck, the deck on which I traveled the Atlantic on the Mary some 60 years earlier. First things first, however - where do we eat! There is no problem. The ship/hotel had restaurants, snack bars, novelty shops, souvenir shops and an ice cream parlor. The general public could inspect the ship during designated hours.

Lu and I roamed the ship from stem to stern, looking, taking pictures and having a grand old time. Nothing that I saw, however, reminded me of the old wartime voyage. I know exactly where I slept in '43 (Promenade Deck, starboard side, ship's former library), but no indication of the location was there now. It had been converted to a snack bar.

The next day we took the guided tour of the ship. The general public paid for the privilege, but we hotel patrons received it for free. When I told the guide that I had been on the ship many years earlier, he was very interested, asking about some of the details. At one point when the group had congregated in a suitable spot, he told them about this fellow who had cruised in '43 - me. I told them a few things that came to mind and received an unexpected round of applause from them. I really did feel proud.

Other days we visited the fine marine museum in Long Beach, a fancy restaurant south of Long Beach, a nifty swimming pool in a neighboring hotel and, finally, got our tickets for a launch trip ("26 miles across the sea") to Santa Catalina Island off the coast at Long Beach. I had previously searched the literature and found a "Lori's Good Stuff" as a place to eat there. Since Lori is my second cousin's name, I made a connection. We found the place, had some sandwiches there, watched the passing scene in this very bustling town of Avalon, mailed some picture post cards at the local post office and took the city tour. It was a lot of fun, believe me.

As a postscript to the trip, I had bought a book "Gray Ghost - the RMS Queen Mary at War" by Steve Harding. It went into detail about all of the Mary's WW II voyages, including mine. But in the busy time of packing for our departure, I inadvertently left it behind. Oh, no! I wanted that book so badly I called from LAX, but had trouble making myself understood apparently. When we got home, I wrote them a letter which they graciously responded to and told me they would send the book to me. They did, and it made us both happy to receive it. It is on my shelf at this moment. Finish the episode Mary.

The QUEEN MARY, Permanently Docked, Long Beach, California

DROVE BY CAR THROUGH CUMBERLAND GAP, KENTUCKY - 2003

Lu and I decided to go the Elderhostel route this year. We read their catalog which is very thorough and opted for a stay in eastern Kentucky near Corbin, north of Knoxville, Tennessee.

Why Kentucky? Primarily, it was a one-overnight stop drive to get there. Then, Lu had never been to the state and I hadn't been since '58 when I drove through it with my father. Finally, the focus of study was to be the eastern Kentucky folklore, mores and economy. It all seemed interesting. Side trips into nature were also on the agenda. We went out one night, for instance, for an "Owl Prowl" (we only saw one).

Other highlights of the trip included a visit to a natural bridge, an inspection of a restored coal mining and processing plant, demonstrations of local loom handicrafts (my father was a hand loom weaver) and a visit to "the highest falls south of Niagara" - Cumberland Falls.

Two other areas of interest on these trips, important but not often mentioned, are our fellow companions - people - and the food. We made friends with an interesting couple, Mr. & Mrs. Douglas Morton of Rock Hill, Connecticut. As to the food at the rustic hotel at which we stayed, it was unexpectantly excellent. I gave my compliments to the cook which I don't often do.

After the five day stay, we went home by way of Alexandria, Virginia where we stayed with Lu's niece and Maid of Honor, Terri Everett. To travel there we went through the famed Cumberland Gap. You hear about the Gap every once in awhile, mostly in connection with colonial days and Davy Crockett times. The highway through the Gap fairly swooped through mountain passes as we came down from the high country in Kentucky to the lower lands in Virginia. Very exhilarating hour or two. In fact, the whole Kentucky sojourn was exhilarating.

At Cumberland Falls, Kentucky

Avalon, Santa Catalina, California

FOUND OWN NAME IN 1930 US CENSUS ENTRY - 6 YEAR OLD RICHARD – 2003

Lu and I stayed for a few days in Alexandria, VA thanks to the hospitality of our hosts. Terri Everett, her professional name, was married to Mark Lewonowsky. Among the many accomplishments of Terri, was her delving into genealogy. She asked Mark (he was off, she was working) to check out some ancestors at the National Archives, Genealogical Section. He asked if I wanted to go along to which I responded positively.

In the past, I had done a lot of work researching my own ancestors at the Archives. This was the first opportunity I had to investigate the 1930 census data. The census data for individuals is not for public viewing for the length of time of an average lifetime - 72 years. So 72 plus 1930 equals 2002. Since this was 2003, the data became public for the first time.

The item I investigated was my own household in New York City in 1930. After a lot of running around getting the proper film cassettes, etc, I finally found the correct one. With proper manipulation of the cassette viewers, I narrowed my search down to the correct area in NYC and street. I knew we lived on Seaman Avenue in Inwood, Manhattan. And suddenly, there she was - the Ward family; head of household Frederick E., wife Minnie Meier, son Richard F., daughter Marian and boarder Anna Meier. The boarder was my Aunt Annie and the sister of my mom. My brother lacked two months from being born!

Two explanatory notes are in order here. The year of the census, 1930, was, of course, the first of the Great Depression years. Having my unmarried aunt in the apartment and presumably helping out with the rent seemed to make economic sense. Additionally, my aunt, two years older than her sister, was a teacher in the New York City school system. Her profession was very close to being depression-proof. I can remember thinking that she was my rich aunt. In later years (she got married in 1934, by the way), she had an excellent retirement annuity as a municipal employee. Her only daughter was my cousin Irene, whom I've mentioned previously.

To return to the point, however, since the availability of the data is 72 years delayed, only people of a certain age - say 80 or higher, are able to say they saw their own decennial census data, assuming they have the inclination and proximity to do the investigation. I was six at the time. Time sure does fly!

CROSSED OVER TAMPA BAY ON SUNSHINE SKYWAY BRIDGE - 2003

Lu and I decided to drive down to Florida to see my brother and sister-in-law again. Of course, we had mutual standing invitations to visit each other. The closest thing to an excuse for the visit was that this year would be their 49th wedding anniversary. Not half bad!

As usual, we had a great time. But going south, I thought it would be an added fillip to the trip to travel somewhat off our intended route to motor across Tampa Bay on the newer Sunshine Skyway Bridge. We were glad we did. Lu seemed to enjoy the detour and I know I consider it one of my life's more unusual events. She took several snapshots of the modern structure while we were moving.

So we went through Tampa, crossed to the Gulf of Mexico side on a "normal" bridge and headed south through St. Petersburg and, finally re-crossed the bay to return to the east side. As to the bridge, the main supports for the suspension cables were tall, slender, single-standing towers. Their delicateness belied their purpose which was to support the weight of the bridge and all that it would carry. The main support cables were golden in color and shined brightly in the Florida sun. Another feature of the bridge was its conformation. It resembled a snake that had just swallowed a pig! The main span was high to permit Tampa Bay shipping to proceed unabated, but the long approaches over the water at each end were not much above the high water mark.

The bridge was under construction from 1982 through 1987, after a pier of the previous bridge at the location was rammed by a ship. That tragic accident caused 35 deaths. We made it over safely and proceeded down to Bill and Jean in Naples.

Sunshine Skyway Bridge, Florida

HAD SHE CRAB SOUP,
HYMAN'S CHARLESTON, S.C.,
AT TABLE BILLY JOEL ONCE ATE - 2003

In November of 2003, we were sort of talked into going on another Caribbean cruise by our friend in the travel agent's office, Clare Trautmann. Part of me wanted to go, but since we had done so much traveling this year, another part of me wanted to cool our heels for awhile. My wife Lu was amenable to the trip, so we went.

The trip did have a new feature for us. We could travel by our own car some 200 miles south to Charleston, S.C. and board the ship (Norwegian Line's Majesty) there. And to make it doubly more convenient, because Lu was having some leg troubles, we had a temporary handicap parking tag. Because of it, the Norwegian Line allowed us to park gratis for the seven day cruise. Very nice indeed.

By the way, Mr. & Mrs. Trautmann were with us on the trip and, although meals were less formal than on the Holland America Line, we had our dinner companions set for the trip.

But to me the most unusual occurrence on the holiday sojourn in November, was roaming Charleston, SC. I was impressed with the city, its architecture, its history, its treatment of visitors, its location on the bay. And its charm. Lu and I had lunch at a restaurant named Hyman's. We were told their she crab soup was excellent. They were right - to me it was heavenly. And to top it all off, we were seated at a table on the second floor; my particular side of the table had a small shiny brasss plaque nailed down which indicated that the old piano man, Billy Joel had eaten there. So what's a decade or two - we both ate at that table. Who knows, he may have enjoyed the she crab soup also!

VIEWED PART OF TRANSIT OF VENUS
ACROSS SOLAR DISK, NC - 2004

One of our eclipse buddies, Randy Shekeruk, sent out an e-mail to his cohorts indicating that the planet Venus was going to be exactly on line between the Sun and the Earth. In other words, we earthlings would be able to see our sister planet Venus silhouetted on the solar disk. At a certain time, we eastern Tarheels would see a black dot move across the fiery Sun. How cool is that!

The event is rather rare, happening roughly every 22 years or so. Occasionally, sightings can be but two years apart provided the sun is above the horizon for any particular viewer and it's not a cloudy day. Randy gave us the timing he obtained to watch in Eastern Standard Time. He lived in Rochester, Minnesota.

Well, Lu and I got up early on June 8th and had our breakfast. We proceeded to drive but a quarter of a mile to park in a relatively clear parking area to await the sunrise. We didn't have long to wait, but we were very apprehensive about some low lying clouds. But once again, Lady Luck was with us; the clouds drifted away and there was the golden old Sol. The air was dense at sunrise enabling us to view the sun directly, but we used our dark eclipse glasses for a safer view.

And there it was - the black dot that was Venus was a little more than halfway across the disk. True, the sighting isn't spectacular, per se, like a solar eclipse, but because of its relative rarity one gets an awesome sense of accomplishing a rare feat. And we didn't have to travel a great distance to take it in!

Let's put this event on our list of unusual happenings.

LEARNED UNUSUAL FACTS ABOUT HORSESHOE CRABS, CHINCOTEAGUE & ASSATEAGUE, VA ELDERHOSTEL - 2004

Lu and I decided to take advantage of Elderhostel again. We very much enjoyed the last one in Kentucky. We wanted to go to a location where one days drive would get us there. We decided on the eastern shore of our neighboring state to the north, Virginia. The focus of the week would be on seashore animal life and the lighthouse at Assateague.

We stayed at a motel in Chincoteague and had our meals in a next door restaurant. Chincoteague is known for the horse swim from Assateague across the channel. Once a year after the swim, the wild horses are corralled and auctioned off to the highest bidder. There are those that disagree with the practice, but it does support the local volunteer fire services. There is a statue in town honoring the famous 'Chincoteague Ponies'.

One evening we were given an assignment to drive to a spot where we could determine the timing of the light from the Assateague Lighthouse. The next day in class we all compared notes and came up with the actual timing. A mariner can determine which beacon he is seeing by checking the on-off light cycle.

Another day we combed the beach looking for marine life and then investigated the wild horses in their natural habitat on Assateague. We also visited several local artists, painters and sculptors, to see them at their craft.

But the most unusual revelation for me was obtained in a lecture one day. The talk was on horseshoe crabs and the fact that they've been on this earth as a species for 350 million years which makes them one of the oldest species still alive. Added to this was the fact that they had blue blood in their bodies. It seems, as ours is red and iron-based, theirs is copper-based which gives the blood a blue color. But the final fact about the lowly sea creature you see washed up on the beach with its spider-like appendages beneath the brown shell or carapace, is that the blue blood contains a substance that when isolated can be used in hospital operating rooms to save lives. This all seemed so unusual to me. The blood is drawn and saved from the creature - the horseshoe crab does not die in the process. By the way, the crab is not a crab at all, but a member of the spider family!

After the week we headed back to our home on the eastern shore of North Carolina. We had to traverse the engineering marvel which is the Chesapeake Bay Bridge-Tunnel Complex. We had our lunch there watching the bay shipping pushing through the choppy channel waters. Loved it! We came home refreshed and a little bit wiser in the ways of the world.

PLAYED IN SURF ON OCRACOKE ISLAND, NC - 3RD BEST BEACH IN USA - 2004

One warm weekday (or was it hot) my wife Lu and I decided to head for the beach. I mean when you're less than an hour away from the cool Atlantic, what's the problem!

We drove to Morehead City, NC, then Cedar Island where we caught a car-carrying ferry to the Outer Banks, the town of Okracoke on Okracoke Island to be specific. These islands are relatively pencil thin, long and narrow, surrounded by the Atlantic Ocean and Pamlico Sound waters. The ferry trip was fun as I gave the numerous seagulls what they craved - food. They were as thick as thieves. Lu, as she so often does, struck up a conversation with another female passenger.

We arrived in Okracoke in just short of an hour. We found a nice restaurant outside of town to gain some needed sustenance. (The sea air makes you hungry). Then it was on the road again, the road to another ferry and Hatteras Island and the famous lighthouse. But we didn't go to Hatteras; we instead stayed on Okracoke Island and pulled into a public parking area with rest and dressing facilities hard by the Atlantic.

The beach was beautiful. Tan and fine sand and, of course, those relentless combers slapping their way landward. There was beach as far as the eye could see in both directions. This year the beach was designated as the third best beach in the country (Hawaii included) by a guy who makes it his business to judge these things. Okracoke Beach faces southeast and is bound to catch some of those warmer Gulf Stream waters. But with a good day's hot sun, it really doesn't matter.

Lu and I did little more than wet our legs, catch a few rays and walk to where some beach artist was sand-sculpturing. He was making whimsical sprites and sea creatures maybe two feet high. The time soon came when we had to reverse our morning's trip and head home. Since the ferry runs on a fixed schedule, keeping track of the time is quite important. We both enjoyed our beach day so much. It must be done again sometime.

Venerable Assateague Lighthouse, Virginia

Assateague Pony Memorial

Magnificent Ocracoke Beach, North Carolina

Sand Sculptor's Creations, Okracoke, NC

PHOTOGRAPHED, AS WW II VETERAN, AT NEW WW II NATIONAL MEMORIAL, DC - 2004

On our way south after visiting my cousin Irene in Newburgh, NY, we stopped by Lu's niece Terri Everett in Alexandria, VA. I specifically wanted to see, as a WW II veteran, and be photographed at the new World War II National Memorial on the Capitol Mall in Washington, DC.

Terri, her husband Mark, Lu and I all went over the Potomac Bridge to DC one early evening. Right in between the Lincoln Memorial and the Washington Monument was this gleaming white memorial to the soldiers and civilians who worked and sacrificed their lives and their efforts to defeat an enemy dedicated to vanquishing the free world.

The memorial, just to the east of the Lincoln Memorial Reflecting Pool, was composed of two halves - one dedicated to the Atlantic campaigns and the other to the efforts in the Pacific during WW II. For the most part, commemorative groupings were composed of numerous white marble slabs, walls and structures. In the center, water fountains splashed in the central pool. All fifty US states were represented.

Lu and I were photographed in front of the North Carolina structure and I made it a point to be seen in front of the New York location, my birthplace. Terri and Mark, of course, fronted the Virginia marker. President Franklin D. Roosevelt's quotation was inscribed on another tablet.

> "Pearl Harbor, December 7, 1941, a date which will live in
> infamy ... no matter how long it may take us to overcome
> this premeditated invasion, the American people, in their
> righteous might, will win through to absolute victory."

And so, after years of effort, it was accomplished.

And that's the story of the visit to "my" DC monument.

At the New World War II Memorial, Washington, DC

MET PIANIST MAC FRAMPTON (PREVIOUSLY MET ON CRUISE) AT HIS NEW BERN CONCERT - 2004

Lu and I usually attend the season's concert series in New Bern. When we looked over the eight upcoming events, we spied Mac Frampton's name. Mr. Frampton is a virtuoso pianist of mostly popular and contemporary music. He is a showman with an energetic style of playing the instrument.

He was one of the headline acts on our second trip to the Caribbean on the MS RYNDAM in December of 2000. We enjoyed his performance very much. But two days later, in one of those group "meet the artist" discussions, we met the man in the ship's lounge area. I can remember specifically asking him how he acquired his energetic style of piano playing. As I recall, he said that it just evolved as his act evolved. Dumb question, but I wanted to ask him something.

But back to New Bern. As I say, four years later he shows up in our concert series. Won't that be great to get to see him again (not that he would know us from Joe and Mrs. Blow).

So after the well-attended performance at a local high school assembly hall, Lu and I worked our way up to and on to the stage and introduced ourselves. We, of course, told him where we had met him four years earlier. He said he remembered the RYNDAM trip and remembered the two of us at the later question and answer session. Now I know as a couple, Lu and I are rather distinctive because of our colors, but I find it a little hard to believe, with as many adoring fans as he must have over the years, that he truly <u>did</u> remember us. But hey, maybe he did. Anyway, Lu and I went back home very satisfied that cold December evening.

We did receive his autograph and his web address. I eventually wrote him an e-mail thanking him for greeting us, but, alas, I never received a response. That's the end of my Mac Frampton story. The man is still a great entertainer.

RECEIVED SHOCKING NEWS THAT MY NON-SMOKING WIFE LU HAS 4TH STAGE LUNG CANCER - 2005

The day started off like any other day, except Lu had an appointment with an oncologist. We also had to go to a medical facility other than the one we usually go to, to meet him. Other than that, we had no inkling of the news which was about to be imparted to Lu, although seeing a specialist was a bit puzzling to us.

Dr. Abyankar proved to be a very interesting fellow to hold a conversation with. He was from Ohio of Asian Indian ancestry. He was very good-natured with a ready laugh. But his diagnosis of Lu's coughing and tiredness was devastating - lung cancer. He preceded the news by saying that Lu was very fortunate to have reached the ripe old age of 88 (89 in a few weeks) and still be a good-looking woman. He didn't mention any time constraint, but, when pressed, did say that her cancer was fourth stage - and there are only five stages.

I must say it took this news awhile to sink in, at least for me. Maybe this was the denial stage. How could this be? My loving and active wife of eight and a half years, my non-smoking companion had lung cancer. And why didn't our primary care doctor see this coming? Why, why? I've subsequently learned that lung cancer is very difficult to detect much in advance of onset, but still - .

Lu's niece Terri Everett was working in Washington, DC, but she came down to visit us frequently. In fact, she arranged to carry out some of her duties from an office set up for her in Camp Lejeune in nearby Jacksonville, NC. I was a little puzzled by this action, but she said simply that Lu was family - Lu was her "mod" aunt. Needless to say, Terri's assistance was very helpful in this situation. The situation continued for several months as Lu slowly succumbed to her terrible malady.

Why, why?

WON SILVER MEDAL, 5K RACE WALK, 5 NC COUNTY SENIOR GAMES TWO YEARS IN ROW - 2006

As is my habit, I had signed up for participation in the five county (Neuse River) Senior Games. One has to submit an application two months in advance and, in view of our situation, I was conflicted. But, I judged that it would be all right, since no travel, to speak of, was involved. The games were held in New Bern, up the road a few miles. Terri Everett was here and, in addition, we were helped by the services of a volunteer to sit with Lu and to call, if necessary.

My event, the Five Kilometer Race Walk was held in the nearby New Bern High School athletic field. The facilities were excellent. There were only two participants in my event and age group (80 to 84), so I was guaranteed a silver if I finished.

My Sunday morning routine is to walk an hour or 3.5 miles. I've been doing it for years. As a matter of fact, I've been doing it, or better, since 1965 starting in Washington, DC, except for a break or two here and there! So I felt I would have no trouble in this instance. But, the other fellow in our age group, a year younger, was an excellent race walker. He had been in competition as a race walker for years. As he passed me on the track during the race, he was kind enough to give me a few pointers about race walking, but, of course, he easily rated the gold medal and, after finishing, I received the silver. I was proud of the medal. We picked them up at a later date.

My times in minutes were 55 in '05 and 53 in '06 so at least there was an improvement.

FOUND OUT WIFE LU HAD DIED WHILE I WAS ON A LOCAL ERRAND - 2006

My wife Lu was diagnosed with lung cancer in early December of '05. She was able to conduct somewhat of a normal life for several months, but at a reduced pace. As a matter of fact, she and I went to Atlantic Beach on the coast in March of '06 where we stayed for two nights at a motel. She didn't feel like doing too much, but I'm sure she enjoyed doing some of the things we used to do in happier days.

By April, however, she stayed quite a bit in bed. Occasionally she would talk strangely. One night she sat at the foot of the bed and folded and refolded a towel for hours. I had slipped off to sleep only to awake to see her at the same activity.

Another night when we were alone, I had to call the emergency medical team. Somehow she had slipped out of the bed and was lying on the floor. I tried but could not get her back on the bed. She seemed so heavy to me at that time, although she was not a particularly heavy woman.

Of course, during these months, she had many, many visitors - mostly relatives, neighbors and friends. She was loved by anyone who met her. Her pastor and assistants came by one afternoon. I think - I know she enjoyed seeing all those people. Terri and her husband Mark came down from Alexandria and stayed in our guest room for a few days. Of course, her niece, Terri, was there often.

But on May 18, 2006, I had gone to the Recycle Center in the morning to discard trash, and garden and lawn vegetation. The nurse from the Hospice Care organization was with her as was Terri. When I got back, Terri met me in the garage and told me that Lu, her dear Aunt Lu, was gone. It hit me like a ton of bricks. The nurse called the authorities. My Lu is gone.

> "No motion has she now, no force.
> She neither hears nor sees.
> Rolled 'round in earth's diurnal course,
> With rocks, and stones and trees."
>
> Wm. Wordsworth

SPOKE AT LU'S FUNERAL AT HER CHURCH IN JACKSONVILLE, NC, - 2006

My wife's funeral was held at Marshall Baptist Church in Jacksonville, NC. I certainly didn't look forward to this day, but I had a duty to perform and I followed through with it.

The church was filled to overflowing with so many of Lu's relatives and friends. As background, Lu's mother was well known throughout the area as Ma Phebe. She lived with vigor throughout her lifetime and died in 1988 at the age of 98. And it so happens Ma Phebe's mother, Lu's maternal grandmother of course, also died at the age of 98. I think Lu expected to live to that age at least.

The church was attended by mostly black people. The service was an open-casket ceremony. I as the husband spoke first after the church officials. I tried to be as simple, honest and direct as I could. Many of these people had known Lu and the other members of the Burnett family for many years.

I spoke to how we met after her cousin Thelma Martin passed away, how Lu and I conducted a courtship at a 350 mile distance at first, how we had the handicap of our racial differences and the fact that we were both on the verge of being octogenarians, how we married out-of-doors in a Washington, DC condominium complex, and the way she accompanied me on many exotic trips through the USA, the Caribbean and Europe. I added the fact that we acquired and raised two cats as our "children" and enjoyed our morning walks around the Washington, DC area and our trips to her family reunions and mine. Terri her niece was at my side at the podium since, at first, I was a bit teared up and nervous. I concluded the short remarks by stressing that the cats and I would now go on without our mother and wife.

But all went well judging from the comments and compliments I received later. I kissed Lu on the cheek prior to the ride to the cemetery where she would be buried. At the cemetery service, other kind words were spoken. She was buried next to her mother, Ma Phebe, and step-father. Terri had suggested the release of doves to conclude the ceremony. Several months later, I had Lu's stone emplaced. Besides the customary name and dates, I called her "Our Angel" because that was what she was to me and her friends and relatives. She truly was an angel.

MET WITH FELLOW ECLIPSE CHASER ON BATTLESHIP "NORTH CAROLINA" IN WILMINGTON, NC - 2007

One of the eclipse chasers from our old group was Randy Shekeruk (accent on the second syllable). The man is a bachelor and works for IBM in Rochester, Minnesota. We correspond sporadically by e-mail, although he does most of the corresponding, I'm afraid. He's really a remarkable fellow.

I guess you'd call him a renaissance man - he's into anything interesting. He not only follows eclipses and has been to more of them than I have, he keeps track of the total minutes he has been in the moon's shadow - lifetime! He keeps his fellow eclipse freaks (like me) informed about future astronomical events. He's chased eclipses in Australia, South Africa, on the Black Sea, Egypt and in the central Pacific, plus some of the later ones we've seen as a group in Uruguay and the Caribbean. He also is a big blood donor, having donated, I don't know, ten gallons in his lifetime or some other amazingly high amount.

Anyway, he called me one day from Myrtle Beach, SC. One of his other accomplishments, you see, is to spend at least a night in every US state. South Carolina completed his ambitious feat. He was on a golfing vacation. I suggested we meet someplace between Myrtle Beach and New Bern, NC. I suggested the battleship NORTH CAROLINA docked in Wilmington, NC. He readily agreed for a day that wouldn't interfere with his golfing schedule.

This would be my first significant trip since Lu's death. Lu kept wanting me to go with her to the battleship, but I kept putting it off. I finally made it, Lu. I guess I was glad to be on the road again if only for 100 miles or so.

Although he was late, we took the tour of the WW II leviathan ship. North Carolina school children had something to do with saving the proud naval vessel from the salvage yard. They donated their small change to the cause. There was a lot to see on the steel ship.

Later, we had dinner at a fine restaurant in Wilmington where we talked over old times. I hadn't seen him in nine years since the 1998 total solar eclipse trip in the Caribbean off Guadeloupe. Of course, he was shaken when he had heard about Lu in an e-mail I sent him last year.

After dinner and further conversation, we parted, he south, I north. I was back in bed in New Bern that night. I think the trip was therapeutic for me. I really enjoyed doing something a bit out of the ordinary and non-routine again.

DROVE NEW BERN, NC TO NEAR ROANOKE, VA, THEN TO ALEXANDRIA, VA, - 2007

ON WAY HOME FROM ALEXANDRIA HAD CAR ACCIDENT

On my next step to come out of the funk of my wife Lu's death, I decided to take another Elderhostel trip. This one would take me to western Virginia, in the Allegheny foothills, to Smith Mountain Lake. The lake is actually the backup waters of the Smith Mountain Dam. The area is a beautiful locality attracting many fine homes and recreational facilities.

The Elderhostel trip took me to a nature facility near the lake that had private sleeping accommodations in a barracks-like setting. The focus of the four day learning experience was digital cameras, how to use them, how to print photos through the computer. I had recently purchased one and was interested in learning more about the devise. During the week we also took side trips on the lake itself and to the dam. Other trips included a very interesting railroad museum in Roanoke and Booker T. Washington's childhood home and farm. The group, about two dozen of us, had engaging and educational sessions.

Instead of going directly home to New Bern, NC, I drove to Alexandria, VA where I stayed with Terri (Lu's niece) and Mark for a couple of days. She had offered me a standing invitation to come and stay with them. They had a three-story townhouse on the Potomac. It was a beautiful area. I enjoyed the stay and took the opportunity to thank Terri for all she had done to help me during Lu's final months and afterwards.

Soon, it was time to head home. I got within 35 miles of New Bern and, while my attention was distracted while looking for a place to eat near Washington, NC, I rear-ended a car going at a slow speed. My airbags deployed and I felt bad - mentally. There were no injuries to me or to two members of the other car. But my front end submarined below the other car's rear end. My engine was done for.

The authorities soon came, took notes and helped me get in touch with my neighbors (Jim Higgins and Ruth Rinka) back in New Bern who came and picked me up. I had to appear in court in Washington, NC later in the month, but, on proof of insurance, I was told I was free to go. That was very good news.

Except for the final incident, the whole sojourn was everything I could ask for. I enjoyed almost all of it!

DRANK PEPSI-COLA AT BIRTHPLACE OF DRINK IN NEW BERN, NC WITH WOMAN MET ON INTERNET - 2007

More than a year after my wife Lu's death, I spied a lady's picture on the internet that seemed to me was worth corresponding with. She was from my former area in the Washington, DC vicinity, namely, Woodbridge, VA. We struck up a very good electronic conversation. I looked forward to becoming better acquainted. She was a widow with grown children living away from her. She did talk a lot about her (one of her?) granddaughters whom she took to the stores and the beach occasionally.

Her name was Bettye Shiflett. One day she surprised me by calling me on the phone. I suppose I had given her my number, but I don't remember doing so. She was an intelligent woman of 77 who had been in a job that involved writing and travel. She was somewhat familiar with the New Bern area and expressed interest in visiting the North Carolina town. I guess I was anxious to have us meet; the internet is fine, but there is nothing like a face-to-face encounter to become more acquainted.

She did make arrangements to stay at a nearby motel, but the motel was difficult to get to because of major repair work being done on a bridge in the vicinity. I talked her into staying in my guest room and saving some money in the bargain which she did. To get to the point, we met, she stayed at my place, we talked, but nothing proceeded any further. The next day we went into New Bern and saw some of the historical parts of the city - the Tryon Palace, a restored colonial administrative building - and the drug store where the Pepsi-Cola drink was invented in the 1890's. We sat at the counter, had a Pepsi and talked with the current proprietor who was a very interesting fellow. It was a lot of fun.

But, we really didn't hit it off. She seemed a little up-tight to me. She talked about her family quite a bit. She was a diabetic and I think we mutually agreed to put the brakes on the relationship. Of course, it's difficult to end any affair, mild as it was, but I think it was the right thing to do. Too bad but so be it.

CANOED TRENT RIVER, POLLOCKSVILLE TO NEW BERN, NC IN PERFECT WEATHER - 2007

As a widower, I had to change my life quite a bit. Everybody tells me that there is a danger for men in my position to neglect their social life and become reclusive. This is one of the reasons I became more acquainted with "The Friends of River Bend".

River Bend is, you might say, a suburb of New Bern and it is where Lu and I lived. It's almost completely residential. The Friends of River Bend is a group of ecology-minded people who want to assure that the town adopts rules and regulations that are in tune with a natural environment. Among their activities is the encouragement of nature walks and the maintenance of paths for those walks.

This summer they sponsored an annual canoe and kayak trip downstream on a local and picturesque river. Although I was 84 this year, I thought I could do it and have fun doing it. I signed up. We didn't have to have our own boats. We carpooled to Pollocksville, NC some seven miles southwest.

I originally wanted a kayak (crew of one), but had to settle for a canoe. I asked some nice looking lady if she were canoeing and if she had a partner. She too was looking for a canoeing partner. Lucky me!

So off we went - waiting first for the group of 20 or 30 people to get into their boats. They took some pictures which appeared later in the local River Bender newspaper. It was somewhat awkward at first to coordinate her actions in the front of the canoe with mine in the rear and go straight forward, but we got the hang of it soon enough.

Soon we were talking up a storm. Her name was Linda Haven and she was a 53 year old divorcee. She, like me, had traveled quite a bit. She, like me, had lost a spouse, although in a very different way. She, like me, loved nature and animals. So we had much in common. Too bad our ages were a generation apart. Our trip down the Trent River went by very quickly.

After the beautiful but uneventful trip, we all gathered at the River Bend Town Hall to hear some talks and imbibe some light refreshments. But all too soon it was time to depart. I had some pictures taken of Linda and me and, I must say, we made a nice looking couple. We exchanged a few messages on the internet in the days and weeks that followed, but that was the end of the platonic affair. Oh well, there's always tomorrow.

WALKED 5250 MILES IN 10 YEARS, RIVER BEND, NC - 2008

As has been said, walking and keeping records of the time and weather is one of my hobbies. There was a six month hiatus as I changed locations from Washington, DC to River Bend (near New Bern), NC in October 1997. I use a code to identify the weather. On a five point scale (1 is low); I note the wind speed, cloud cover, air density and precipitation. Other identifiers in the string of digits include month, date, temperature and time in minutes for the three and a half mile walk.

Needless to say, I have a lot of records accumulated over the 10 year NC period and the 32.5 year Washington, DC period. In the early days, I obtained IBM cards and metal pins to manipulate the data. That soon gave way in 1984 to the ever-loving computer. That fine invention allowed me to put all my records into the computer and manipulate and print the data to my heart's content with very little effort.

My first recorded NC walk, for instance, was May 31, 1998, temperature 76, light wind, half cloudy, medium air density and no precipitation. My time for the walk was 80 minutes (before I settled on the 3.5 mile distance). Ten years later, the June 1, 2008 walk shows a temperature of 72, partly cloudy, low air density and no rain. The time was 64.5 minutes.

By the way, all the NC walks were done at approximately 8:30 AM. By contrast, the DC walks were performed at about 10:30 AM (I used to drive Thelma to church first and then do my walk or jog). Other tidbits - the hottest walk in NC was August 1, 1999 (85 degrees), the coldest, January 11, 2004 (20). Also, the total miles in the heading includes non-Sunday walks as well, shorter distances but more numerous.

The books aren't closed yet - I'm still a slave to my walking/record keeping hobby. The pace continues!

Some people say that I look sort of good for an 85 year old male. Maybe, but if it's true, I owe it mostly to the 42.5 years of walking and jogging. It can't last too much longer though, darn it. As the months pile up, a few more aches, creaks, imbalances, pains, stiffnesses, tremors and weaknesses (alphabetical order) slowly seem to be rearing their unwanted presence. Well, it is inevitable, I suppose, darn it.

WON RAFFLE AND SOLD HOUSE IN FIRST TWO WEEKS OF DECEMBER - 2008

In the fall, I contributed to an animal-assistance organization, Pals for Paws, by buying five raffle tickets. But surprise, surprise - on December 1, a lady called me to inform me that I had won the raffle! She told me how much the prize was, but I mis-heard her. I thought she said fifty dollars which made me very happy.

You see, at this point in my life I was paying off a mortgage on the house (Lu's and mine) that I had on the market since March and, in addition, paying monthly rent on the apartment I was living in. This double expense, coupled with the lawn care expense of the house, put a genuine strain on my monthly government annuity.

But, people began congratulating me for winning first prize in the raffle. First prize was $300 - not a million, but a nice little number of dollars you must admit.

And then in a few more days, my real estate agent told me, at long last she had a buyer for the house. This was really happy news, although I was getting used to this happy news stuff! At any rate, on December 10, we went to closing. That afternoon I had my proceeds. And Christmas was still two weeks away!

Life is an amazing thing -- full of twists and turns, peaks and valleys, dark tunnels and bright vistas. We can only hope that it will be a long, healthful and productive one for us all.